Desktop Publishing on a Shoestring

with

Ian Sinclair

BSP PROFESSIONAL BOOKS

Copyright © Ian Sinclair 1988

All rights reserved. No part of this
publication may be reproduced, stored
in a retrieval system, or transmitted,
in any form or by any means, electronic,
mechanical, photocopying, recording
or otherwise without the prior
permission of the copyright owner.

First published 1988

British Library
Cataloguing in Publication Data
Sinclair, Ian R. (Ian Robertson),
    Desktop publishing on a shoestring, with
Fleet Street Editor.
    1. Desktop publishing. Applications of
microcomputer systems.
Software packages.
Fleet Street Editor.
I. Title.
070.5′028′55369

ISBN 0–632–02495–X

BSP Professional Books
A division of Blackwell Scientific
    Publications Ltd
Editorial Offices:
Osney Mead, Oxford OX2 0EL
    (Orders: Tel. 0865 240201)
8 John Street, London WC1N 2ES
23 Ainslie Place, Edinburgh EH3 6AJ
3 Cambridge Center, Suite 208, Cambridge
    MA 02142, USA
667 Lytton Avenue, Palo Alto, California
    94301, USA
107 Barry Street, Carlton, Victoria 3053,
    Australia

Set by DP Photosetting, Aylesbury, Bucks
Printed and bound in Great Britain by
the Alden Press, Oxford

Contents

Preface   iv
1   What Is Desktop Publishing?   1
2   Getting Started   23
3   More Text Techniques   43
4   Starting With Graphics   64
5   Advanced Techniques   90
6   Final Words   115
Appendix A: Fleet Street Editor and Machines   130
Appendix B: Some Useful Addresses   132
Appendix C: Laser Printers and Page-description Languages   134
Index   136

Preface

Desktop publishing is by this time well established, and there are many packages and books for the large-scale user who has no qualms at spending sums of the order of £7000 on equipment, and several hundred pounds per month on running costs. For each user in that category, however, there are ten whose means and requirements are considerably more modest. Items as diverse as church newsletters, Bob-a-Job Week leaflets, menus for the small cafe or hand-out advertising sheets for the ironmongers; all are candidates for desktop publishing techniques, but not at the prices that are associated with laser printers and expensive computers. It is to this majority group of users who need low-cost desktop publishing that this book is addressed.

Inevitably, some assumptions have to be made. This book has been written while using the well-known desktop publishing program Fleet Street Editor from Mirrorsoft, along with an Amstrad PC 1512 computer and an Epson RX80 printer, all low-cost equipment. The version tested is the one that will run on any IBM PC or compatible which has the minimum requirements of 512K memory and two disk drives. Many readers or potential readers of this book will use the earlier Amstrad PCW 8256 or PCW 8512 models (the PCW 9512 is suitable only if the dot-matrix printer is available), or the CPC 6128 model, and though the setting up steps to run the software will be different, the general use of Fleet Street Editor will follow the same lines. The version of Fleet Street Editor for the PCW machine is, in fact, enhanced in some ways as compared to Version 2 on the PC 1512/PC1640 machines. At the time of writing, V.3.0 of Fleet Street Editor had been announced but was not yet available in final form. This book has been written using V.2.0, but the additional facilities offered by V.3.0 have been noted. There is also a version, considerably enhanced, for the Atari ST computer, called Fleet Street Publisher, and since this follows the same basic pattern as Fleet Street Editor, this book is also suitable as a guide to Desktop publishing on the Atari.

One of the main problems about desktop publishing is that it tends to present the user with a rich choice of styles and fonts, sizes and facilities, graphics and commands. The result of this can be printed work that confuses the eye and is difficult to read. The use of a simple dot-matrix printer rather

Preface

than the expensive laser printer will always result in work that is less visually satisfactory, but if the user resists the temptation to try every special effect that is available, the results can still be very satisfying. Though no book can ever teach the art of typography, the emphasis here is on good-looking results, even if this means that many users will never require more than a few of the huge number of facilities that Fleet Street Editor offers. In the course of this book, however, the full range of these possibilities is explored.

Many buyers of Fleet Street Editor will have had considerable experience with their chosen computer (the package is available for the BBC machines as well as for the Amstrad range), but, equally, many who read this book will not be well versed in the use of MS-DOS and directories. The intitial pages are therefore aimed at the newcomer to the use of the PC 1512/PC 1640 and PPC 640 type of machines, showing how best to make use of the Fleet Street Editor disks. These pages are applicable to most users of **IBM PC-compatible** machines. The user of the earlier Amstrad machines equipped with CP/M will find setting-up instructions applicable to each individual machine in the manual for each specific version. As always, the user of a hard disk machine can make use of the software package most easily, and any reader who is contemplating the addition of a hard disk drive to an Amstrad or similar PC-compatible should consult my book *The Amstrad PC Hard Disk Guide* on this topic. My own copy of Fleet Street Editor was used from a hard disk in the course of preparing this book, but twin-floppy disk owners have not been forgotten, and directions pertaining to disk use will specify what has to be done when using Fleet Street Editor from a twin-drive machine.

I am most grateful to Pat Bitton at Mirrosoft for her support and for the loan of a copy of Fleet Street Editor V.2.0, and for the four sets of additional disks of Executive Fonts, Decorative Fonts, Religious Images and Humorous Images which can be added to enhance the uses of the program. I am grateful also, as always to Richard Miles of BSP who commissioned this book, and to Sue Moore for her indefatigable work on the manuscript.

Ian Sinclair
September 1988

The names *Fleet Street Editor*, *Fleet Street Editor Plus* and *Fleet Street Publisher* are trademarks of Mirrorsoft Ltd.

Names of individuals and organisations that appear in the examples in this book are wholly fictitious. Any resemblance to the name of any person, living or dead, or organisation past or present is purely coincidental.

Also by Ian Sinclair

The Amstrad PC Hard Disc Guide
0 632 02291 4

Lotus Agenda
0 632 02336 8

LocoScript 2
0 632 02185 3

Communications with the Amstrad PC
0 632 02292 2

Use Your Ability – Including Ability Plus
0 632 02231 0

Chapter One
What Is Desktop Publishing?

Desktop publishing, or DTP, is the name for low-cost publishing, using a computer and its associated printer to prepare material which can be used as a master for further printing work, or to make a limited number of copies of the material directly. Prior to the desktop publishing revolution, anyone who needed material to be published had the options of duplicating typed material, using ink duplicators (the familiar Roneo and Gestetner machines), photocopiers, or offset litho machines; or using the services of a local printer to lay out type. At one time, anyone needing printed material of reasonable standard who wanted to take the do it yourself approach could do so only by way of a hand-press, such as the excellent Adana range. Many Adana owners learned much about typography in this way (I was one very satisfied Adana owner), but the time that is needed to assemble type for much more than a visiting card can be prohibitive, and fonts of type are quite costly.

The use of a computer allows typography to be handled in very much the same way as word processing. This means that the form of the printed material can be seen on the screen and manipulated as much as you like in this form without a single mark being made on paper. Each page of the work can be completed and recorded on disk, and only when the whole set of pages is ready need anything be printed. The page can contain text that uses different forms of type (different *fonts*), in different sizes that allow you to have headlines, sub-headings, main text and notes, along with graphics illustrations that you can prepare for yourself or which you can take ready-made from a selection that comes with the desktop publishing package or on additional disks. The pictures from these sources can be placed into the page, with the words of the text making way for them and arranged around them as you choose. Both text and pictures are then printed together, with no need for the pasting-up processes that will be familiar to anyone who has worked with a mixture of text and graphics, or even with text material that has required insertions.

Essential equipment

The essential equipment for desktop publishing comprises a computer, a printer, and the necessary software program. If you were considering buying a computer specially for desktop publishing, and had no other use for the machine, then it would make sense to buy a machine that featured a very clear and finely detailed screen display, such as the Atari ST. In this book, however, I am making the assumption that you already use a computer, and that your computer has been bought for business purposes or for hobby use to run programs such as word processors, spreadsheets and databases (as distinct from games). This makes it likely that you are using either a PC-compatible machine, like the Amstrad PC 1512, PC 1640 or PPC 640, or one of the Amstrad PCW machines such as the PCW 8256, PCW 8512, or possibly the CPC 6128. Fortunately, there is one desktop publishing program which is available in (slightly different) forms for all these machines, and which is also available (enhanced) for the Atari ST and in a rather different form for the BBC Micro (although the limited memory of the older BBC machine makes the use of desktop publishing rather difficult).

The printer has been assumed to be a low-cost 9-pin dot-matrix printer such as the Epson RX/FX range, and the examples in this book have all been printed on an elderly Epson RX80. There is a huge variety of printers of this type made by several manufacturers, and all compatible with the Epson. If you are buying a printer, as distinct from making use of an existing printer, then you should find out the costs of spare ribbons before deciding, because many printers that are sold at prices lower than that of a compatible Epson will cost considerably more to use in terms of ribbon prices. The important point, however, is that if you have a printer that is an Epson or is Epson-compatible, along with a suitable computer and software, then you can start desktop publishing work. Users of the Amstrad PCW 8256 and PCW 8512 will have the Amstrad printer which accompanies these machines, and the version of Fleet Street Editor, called Editor Plus, that you use will be able to make use of that printer. If you want to make use of other printer types with the machines, you need an add-on, the parallel-serial port. Users of the PCW 9512 will have the daisywheel printer which is not suitable for desktop publishing use, but they can add a dot-matrix printer.

If, of course, you are using the more costly 24-pin type of dot-matrix printer, such as the Epson LQ500, NEC Pinwriter P2200, or Amstrad LQ5000DI models, you can obtain printouts of your desktop publishing pages that are of rather better quality (and are produced more rapidly) than from the simpler 9-pin printers. Fleet Street Editor allows you to make full use of these printers, and the latest V.3.0 of Fleet Street Editor also permits you to use the built-in fonts of these printers as you please, rather than requiring the shape of the lettering to be specified directly by the computer. The older V.2.0 does not allow for built-in printer fonts.

Because this book is concerned with the user who needs desktop publishing on a shoestring (and possibly also in spare time), laser printers are not of primary concern in this edition. The rate at which the cost of laser printers is falling, however, means that in a year or so the cost of purchasing and using a laser printer might well be within the reach of a small business or a large church, even within the reach of a scout or cub group. Certainly if your published material is photocopied, and you need to replace the photocopier, it would make considerable sense to consider replacing the photocopier with a laser printer, since the machines are basically similar, and use the printer to make multiple copies of your desktop publishing pages rather than making a master from a dot-matrix printer and then photocopying this master. Much depends on the numbers of your publication that you need. For a church magazine or other newsletter with a limited circulation, this type of use of a photocopier or a laser printer is ideal, but for other applications, like making advertising 'fliers', visiting cards, or widely-circulated advertising newsletters it would make more sense to stick to the making of a master copy and use these as 'camera-ready copy' for offset litho or other printing techniques. Chapter 6 contains further details of the techniques that you can use to make multiple copies (reprography) of your master copies.

Word processing and desktop publishing

Perhaps you already make use of a word processing program. If you do, you might at this point wonder what precisely is the difference between a word processed document and one that has been produced by desktop publishing. The answer depends very much on what you expect to do. If your requirements are simply for text that can be read, replacing the use of a typewriter and duplicator, then it's quite likely that a straightforward word processor program would do all that you want. The more you want to make use of different fonts of lettering and graphics effects, the less likely that a word processing program can cope. Even quite simple requirements in this respect can make it necessary to have a word processor that is far from cheap, probably costing more than the desktop publishing package that we shall be using. If you want to create pages that look like newspaper pages or advertisement leaflets, then it's most unlikely that a word processor can cope, and desktop publishing is the only sensible way to go. That said, there is no doubt that many of the top-price word processor programs are making more and more use of desktop publishing techniques – but at a high price.

An illustration shows very much better what the differences can be. Figure 1.1 is a simple piece of text which we can imagine is a leaflet from your local greengrocer. This has been produced using a word processor and printed on a daisywheel printer. The text is fully justified, meaning that the lines of text have an even right-hand margin rather then the ragged margin that you get with a typewriter, in addition to the normal even left-hand margin. It's an

<pre>
                    OUR NEW LINES

1. Pickled Walnuts. These are of the finest quality and simply must be
tasted to be believed. We'll have a very special price for you on
Monday, too.

2. Babacos. The exotic fruits come, believe it or not, from the lovely
Island of Guernsey, and are flown here fresh each day. They are of the
Papaya family, but no comparison with other fruits can convey their
taste. Another bonus is that practically every part of the fruit is
edible - no waste.

3. Carambolas. More often called 'Starfruits' because of their shape,
these are another exotic flavour for your table. Like the Babaco,
practically all of the Carambola is edible, and the flavour is a
remarkable combination of citric and pineapple, with a hint of perfume.
Try one with some double cream!
</pre>

Fig. 1.1 A leaflet example, prepared with a word processor and a daisywheel printer (reduced in size to fit this book).

acceptable piece of text, but it is no more visually interesting than a letter from a solicitor. The only effects are the use of underlining and bold (dense black) type, effects that any word processor can produce with any printer, but because of the use of a daisywheel printer, there is no variation in the print size or style. This, I should point out, is not inevitable, because you *can* get other type sizes on a daisywheel printer by changing the printwheel. This, however, demands the use of a word processing program that contains a command that will stop the printing at the correct place so that you can change the daisywheel. You have to remember which wheel to put in each time the printer stops, and word processors such as WordStar Professional 4 can deliver screen messages to remind you of what needs to be done. It's a fiddly process, though, and it's worth remembering that WordStar Professional 4 is an expensive program by modern standards.

Now take a look at Figure 1.2. This makes use of the same text, but has been composed (again on a word processor) so as to be printed on a dot-matrix printer, in this example the Epson RX-80. It is considerably more eye-grabbing, with the use of the large wide lettering on the headline, the smaller bold print for sub-titles, and the smallest print for the actual text. If this is as much as you need, then why use desktop publishing? The answer is simple – work like this on a word processor can take a remarkably long time to set up. You have to remember that with all but a few word processors what you see is not, alas, exactly what you get. My word processor does not show any of the different text sizes, so that centring the headline (Our New Lines) was not simply a matter of pressing the centring key. Instead, a bit of cut and try had to be used, along with calculations based on the size of letters. The main text is printed using 12 characters per linear inch, but the headline uses 5 per inch, so that each large character takes the space of 2.4 normal characters. Until

```
           OUR  NEW  LINES

1. Pickled Walnuts.

These are of the finest quality and simply must be tasted to be believed.
We'll have a very special price for you on Monday, too.

2. Babacos.

The exotic fruits come, believe it or not, from the lovely Island of
Guernsey, and are flown here fresh each day. They are of the Papaya family,
but no comparison with other fruits can convey their taste. Another bonus
is that practically every part of the fruit is edible - no waste.

3. Carambolas.

More often called 'Starfruits' because of their shape, these are another
exotic flavour for your table. Like the Babaco, practically all of the
Carambola is edible, and the flavour is a remarkable combination of citric
and pineapple, with a hint of perfume. Try one with some double cream!
```

Fig. 1.2 The same leaflet, this time printed with a dot-matrix printer and making use of different type sizes. (Reduced in size.)

you have considerable experience, you will be forced into a long session of trial and error each time you want to produce something new.

In addition, there is a lot that cannot be done. The use of the 9-pin dot-matrix printer gives lettering whose quality is not really very satisfactory, particularly on the headline. The fact that you cannot see the appearance of the finished page on the screen makes it difficult to decide how the work is going without printing a test page. You can easily end up with four test pages for each final version. Above all, though, you simply cannot make the work look anything like a printed page, you can only make it look like something from a rather superior typewriter. This is because printers, like typewriters, use even spacing between letters. Letters vary in width from slim (like i) to fat (like m), and using a uniform spacing makes the i's too far apart and the m's too close. We can read the words with no problem, but the effect is unsatisfactory. Some word processors allow you to adjust the spacing (proportional spacing), but many do not. Even if you *can* use proportional spacing, with the space between letters varying with the width of the letters, the letter *font* is often unsatisfactory, particularly from a 9-pin dot-matrix printer.

'Font' is a word that is rather poorly defined, and you will read several different definitions. To avoid conflicts, we'll use 'font' in the sense that Fleet Street Editor uses it. A font is a letter set, comprising the full set of letters in a range of styles sizes, but all of one design. Design in this sense means the shape of letters, and it's something that you probably have never been aware of unless you have taken an interest in printing. You will, however, have noticed the difference if your daily paper changed its font (as *The Guardian* did in the latter years). Each font design can exist in several *styles*, such as normal, bold and italic. The letters of the alphabet have no real fixed shape, and over the years many typographers and designers (notably Eric Gill) have had very strong opinions as to how these letters should look. A few minutes spent with some old newspapers (from 1940 back) will soon convince you that fashion plays quite a large part in our preferences for type fonts.

Basically, leaving aside Gothic and other fancy fonts, you will be using fonts that are either normal or sans serif. The serif is a tiny foot or hook at the tips of letters, and omitting this serif leads to a type that looks plainer (more like typewriting) and, to some eyes, more modern. (The font chosen by the publisher for the text of this book, for instance, is Times, a normal typeface, but Helvetica, a sans serif typeface, has been used for headings and figure captions.) Others claim that the sans serif typefaces tire the eye, that they are unpleasant unless used sparingly. This illustrates an important point, that typography is a matter of taste, and no-one can give more than the most vague pointers to good taste in this respect. What we shall try to do is to show what is very definitely not good taste and it is regrettable that most of the worst examples are to be found in desktop publishing-prepared advertisements in the magazines that deal with computing. On the other hand, if your readers

 OUR NEW LINES

1. Pickled Walnuts. These are of the finest quality and simply must be tasted to be believed. We'll have a very special price for you on Monday, too.

2. Babacos. The exotic fruits come, believe it or not, from the lovely island of **Guernsey**, and are flown here fresh each day. They are of the Papaya family, but no comparison with other fruits can convey their taste. Another bonus is that practically every part of the fruit is edible – no waste.

3. Carambolas. More often called '**Starfruits**' because of their shape, these are another exotic flavour for your table. Like the Babaco, practically all of the Carambola is edible, and the flavour is a remarkable combination of citric and pineapple, with a hint of perfume. Try one with some double cream!

Fig. 1.3 The leaflet produced by the aid of Fleet Street Editor, showing the use of graphics and different type fonts.

like all your newsletter to be in a decorative font, who am I to suggest otherwise?

Now take a look at Figure 1.3. This contains the same information, but the style is noticeably different. The waving palms are eye-catching, and suggest the exotic fruits, some of which is on offer. The headline is large, much larger than could be obtained by word processing techniques, and the text is of a much more dense black than would be normal from word processed output. This copy is of a quality that could be used as 'camera-ready copy' by a printer to make thousands of copies at a low price (because there is no charge for making up the master copy).

Until you have some experience, some of the other changes are less obvious. This example has used three different type faces or fonts. One has been used for the headline, another for the sub-headings (names of fruits) and a third for the main text. This is not just a matter of size, though three different sizes have also been used. The letter shapes are different for the three fonts, and until you have some experience with fonts, it can be difficult to see these differences. In each font, you can usually have three styles, normal, italic and bold (some offer also bold italic), and the bold has been used for emphasis. Some typographers would say that the effects have been overdone here, but in a piece of advertising throwaway like this, a little over-emphasis is justified.

We can sum up the differences between desktop publishing and word processing, then, by saying that word processing is a development of typing, but desktop publishing is a development of printing. When you work with desktop publishing, you are creating copy as it would in times past have been created by metal type, but with a fraction of the effort. The example of Figure 1.3 was done in rather less time than the word processed example of Figure 1.2, because so many of the items that need cumbersome adjustments when you use a word processor are done automatically by a good desktop publishing program.

The software

As you will have gathered, the software of desktop publishing is all-important. Unless this software is good, the amount of effort that will be needed to create the effect that you want will be prohibitive, discouraging you from experimenting. As it is, one discouragement to the user of a dot-matrix printer is the time that is needed to print one page in top quality. The V.3.0 of Fleet Street Editor is considerably faster than V.2.0 in this respect, though if you simply want to see what your copy looks like on paper, you can opt for a rough draft which will be printed much more rapidly. There is no low cost answer to the low speed of high quality printing and the high cost answer that *does* exist, the use of a laser printer, is debarred by the conditions we have laid down in this book, of working on a shoestring. Even if you have a ten-page magazine to prepare, however, this time is not really prohibitive as compared to the older methods of typing and pasting-up.

There is a fairly large choice of software for desktop publishing on any machine that is closely compatible with the IBM PC, such as the Amstrad PC, and there is an equally good choice on machines with superior graphics screens, such as the Apple Mac, the Atari ST and the Commodore Amiga. The choice narrows considerably if you want desktop publishing on the Amstrad PCW machines, and is almost non-existent for some machines with limited memory. If you want to find a good package which exists in several versions for various machines and is available at a very reasonable price, comparable with a low-cost word processor, then Fleet Street Editor is virtually the only choice.

All desktop publishing packages are complicated in the sense that there is a lot to learn before you can make really effective use of them. Fleet Street Editor is a good program in the sense that you can obtain relatively simple layouts with ease, and still have little trouble in producing much more ambitious work. The ease with which the software can be used encourages you to experiment and so learn from experience. The lack of an index to some copies of the manual can be a problem, which this book can remedy and which is alleviated in V.3.0 by having on-screen help available for all actions. Ease of use is very important because the small-scale user of desktop publishing will not be running the desktop publishing package every day. Some programs present problems because in the interval between using them once and then returning to them you have forgotten the commands.

Of mice and keys

The PC version of Fleet Street Editor can make use of the mouse that is supplied with the Amstrad PC. If you are using the Amstrad PC and have the mouse, then you will find it an advantage to use it. You are not committed to the use of a mouse, and if you do not use yours, then you can make use of F-keys in place of mouse action. If you are using a PC-compatible which has no mouse, you will be forced to make use of the F-keys in any case, unless you buy and fit a suitable mouse. Users of the Amstrad PCW machines can make use of the F-keys and other specialised keys of those machines, but a mouse is available as an add-on. Fleet Street Editor is helpful in this respect by showing on-screen the keys that have to be pressed in order to simulate mouse action.

The manual for Fleet Street Editor shows for each action the alternative keys to substitute for mouse actions. The convenience of using a mouse for desktop publishing work, however, is such that I cannot imagine any user of

What Is Desktop Publishing? 9

the Amstrad PC wanting to dispense with it when running Fleet Street Editor, no matter how you felt about it for other tasks. In this book, the actions of preparing copy have been described making use of the mouse, rather than to make the descriptions cumbersome by adding a non-mouse method each time. This means that you have to come to grips with a piece of terminology that is peculiar to Fleet Street Editor, the 'half-click'. This is the term that is used for what other books describe as 'mouse dragging', in which you press down the mouse button (left hand button) and hold it while moving the mouse, releasing it only when you have moved the mouse to the required position.

If you have used the mouse along with the Gem system on the PC 1512 you should be familiar with these ideas. Many PC users, however, may have bought the PC for running business programs using MS-DOS and will not have used Gem to any extent. These mouse uses will therefore be unfamiliar, so that all mouse operations will be described fully in the earlier parts of this book, and assumed to be familiar later on.

Making perfect

There is virtually nothing worth doing for which some well-guided practice will not assist in obtaining better results. This is particularly true of desktop publishing, and the more practice you can get, the better able you will be to make effective use of all the equipment and the software. In addition, you need to look at your products critically. Are the points you want to make sufficiently emphasised? Does the page look *interesting*? Would more variation in typeface help, or is the page already a mess because of too many different faces? Could graphics be better used? These are all value judgements, things that cannot be resolved by measurement or mathematics.

Another aspect to practise is that it may be the only way in which you can become acquainted with some aspects of the capabilities of Fleet Street Editor. If, for example, you use desktop publishing to create the menus for a cafe along the road, it's most unlikely that you will learn how to handle the type of work that is required for the Cromwell Club's newsletter. A good principle is to look at other published work, much of which may not have been produced by desktop publishing, and think how you would go about reproducing such pages. Once you learn to think like a printer you are on the way to producing better printed material for yourself. The eye, like the ear, requires education. If you have never heard really excellent hi-fi, for example, you probably have absolutely no idea that such excellence is achievable, but unless you listen to genuinely live music (no microphones, no amplifiers, no loudspeakers) you probably won't appreciate hi-fi. Similarly, unless you learn to appreciate how the pages of a newspaper have been put together and how emphasis has been made, pictures used, headings and sub-headings placed, you are unlikely to be able to produce pleasing results for yourself.

Good technology, as provided by Amstrad, Epson and Mirrorsoft, helps you along the way, but in the final analysis the appearance of your desktop publishing efforts depends on your own eyes, and how critically you use them. In this book, because we are dealing with the shoestring end of desktop publishing, we are looking at black and white text and images only. This is difficult enough, and the addition of colour, available only on very expensive packages, is yet another dimension. Like many males, I am partly colour-blind, and I would not rely on my visual senses to criticise a colour layout. Unless you can make these judgements, your work is not likely to please you, and if it doesn't please you it probably doesn't please anyone else.

Installing Fleet Street Editor

To make effective use of Fleet Street Editor, you need to have the program correctly prepared for use with your machine, the process called installation. If you are using an Amstrad PCW machine, then the set-up instructions are quite specific, the main differences being between the single and the twin disk drives, and the use of 256K or 512K of memory. For the PC type of machine, the steps that you need to take depend rather a lot on the way your computer is equipped, because the IBM PC and a lot of similar machines may have had various graphics card added to them. In this book, I'll assume that you are using the Amstrad PC type of machine, either PC 1512 or PC 1640 because the basic over-the-counter Amstrad has all the circuitry that is needed to make a good job of desktop publishing work with Fleet Street Editor, particularly the PC 1640. If you are using the portable PPC 640, then you *must* use another monitor (some retailers offer a free 12" Ferguson monitor with the PPC 640) because the built-in screen is not suitable for desktop publishing work. This description will also be applicable to most of the modern PC compatibles from sources other than Amstrad.

The main differences in installation, then, concern the differences between twin floppy drive machines and hard disk machines. It is not realistically possible to run Fleet Street Editor with a single $5\frac{1}{4}''$ floppy drive because of the limitation of 360K storage space on a single disk. You *can*, however, use a single drive PPC 640 because the little 3.5" disks hold twice as much data as a single $5\frac{1}{4}''$ disk. If you are using a non-Amstrad PC compatible then you need to be sure that it is fitted with one of the three possible add-on cards that makes desktop publishing display possible on the screen. These would be:

(1) the IBM CGA card, if you use a colour monitor;
(2) the Hercules Graphics card, if you use a monochrome monitor;
(3) the EGA card with a colour monitor.

What Is Desktop Publishing?   11

Note that *very few* colour monitors are really adequate for displaying desktop publishing graphics really well, other than monitors in the £700 price range. For desktop publishing work, a monochrome display is preferable every time, and the better the quality of the monitor the easier it will be for you to see what you are getting. Amstrad owners do not have these worries, but it is again preferable to be using the monochrome rather than the colour monitor.

Fleet Street Editor is distributed on $5 \times 5\frac{1}{4}''$ disks or on $3 \times 3.5''$ disks. As always, you should make backup copies of these disks as soon as you have unpacked them. I shall assume that you are sufficiently familiar with the use of the machine to know what is required in making backups. You can then put the originals away in a safe place, and use the backups to make your working copies, which need not resemble the disks as distributed. Since the procedure differs considerably according to whether you have a hard disk or not, the methods will be described separately.

Hard disk installation

As usual, installation of Fleet Street Editor on a hard disk is considerably easier, as also is the use of the program. At one time, a hard disk was considered as a costly luxury, but with the advent of units like the Western Digital hard disk card, you can add a hard disk to your Amstrad for about £300. In addition, many readers will have bought the hard disk version of the PC 1512 or PC 1640, since more of the hard disk machines are sold than floppy-drive types. The only complication attending the installation of Fleet Street Editor on a hard disk machine is concerned with the use of the AUTOEXEC.BAT file and any other batch file that is used to start Fleet Street Editor.

To transfer the files, assemble the copies of four of the disks, the System disk, Fonts disk, Sampler disk and Graphics Library disk. The entire contents of all four of these disks can be transferred to a directory on the hard disk, and it is convenient, as the Fleet Street Editor manual suggests, to call this directory FSE.

(1) With the machine running, make sure that you are in the root directory by typing CD\ and then pressing RETURN.
(2) Create a directory called Fleet Street Editor by typing MD FSE and then pressing RETURN.
(3) Go to that directory by typing CD FSE and then pressing RETURN.
(4) Place the System disk copy into the floppy drive. Type COPY A:*.* C: and press RETURN.

12 *Desktop Publishing on a Shoestring*

(5) Wait until all of the files have been copied. Remove the System disk and put the Fonts disk in place. Press F3, which will bring up the COPY command again. Pressing RETURN will carry out the copying.

(6) Repeat step 5 with the Sampler disk and the Graphics Library disk. When all the disk files have been transferred, use CD\ (RETURN) to get back to the root directory.

How you make use of these files very much depends on how you use your machine. My own use of the Amstrad PC involves running several different types of files in the course of a day, and when the machine starts up I need to set conditions that will be suitable for all the programs I run. For that reason, no RAMdisk is set, nor is the mouse program, MOUSE.COM run. Figure 1.4(a) shows the AUTOEXEC.BAT file that I use, which is suitable only if the programs SCRNFX and SR are present. You might like to consider the use of the simpler version in Figure 1.4(b). Note that you should not include RAMDRIVE if you have the 512K machine, and even if you have expanded the memory or are using the PC 1640, RAMDRIVE is best omitted.

With this AUTOEXEC.BAT file present, the screen will display a list of BAT files once the machine is up and running. I use a file called DTP.BAT to start up Fleet Street Editor, and its contents are as shown in Figure 1.5. This file runs the MOUSE.COM program, then selects the Fleet Street Editor directory and runs Fleet Street Editor. When Fleet Street Editor finishes, you

```
echo off
path c:\;C:\MSDOS;C:\editors;C:\textutil;c:\ability
keybuk
rtc
prtscfx
sr 200                                                              (a)
dir *.bat
echo on
```

```
echo off
path c:\;C:\MSDOS;C:\FSE
keybuk
rtc                                                                 (b)
dir *.bat
echo on
```

Fig. 1.4 (a) My own AUTOEXEC.BAT file for a hard disk. This uses several programs that you might not have on your disk. (b) A suggested AUTOEXEC.BAT file for a hard disk.

```
echo off
mouse
cd\fse
echo Fleet Street Editor is loading.....
fp
cd\
```

Fig. 1.5 A batch file called DTP.BAT for hard disk use.

will be returned to the root directory, because the batch file ends with cd.

If you have not written batch files, Figure 1.6 is a reminder of how to use the RPED editor program, present on Amstrad distribution disks, to create such a file. Note that there are slight differences between early and later versions of RPED; one uses F10 to delete a line, the other uses Ctrl-Y. If you are using a different brand of PC-compatible then you can use any editor program that provides a file in ASCII code.

Floppy disk installation

One of the problems of using Fleet Street Editor with 5¼" floppy disks is that the discs have a rather limited capacity. This is most noticeable when you are

---

This assumes that RPED is present on the disk you are currently using, or the root directory of your hard disk. If you are using RPED from another drive/directory you must call it using a suitable drive letter or path name, such as B:RPED or \EDITORS\RPED.

(1) Type RPED, followed by a space and then the name of the batch file you want to write. For example, you can use RPED AUTOEXEC.BAT.
(2) When the RPED menu appears, type the lines of the file, using RETURN at the end of each line. Note the keys that have to be used if you want to insert a line or delete a line.
(3) When you have finished, press the ESC key. When you see the menu returning, press the F4 key to leave RPED.
(4) Check that the file in on the disk or directory, and look at the contents using the command TYPE AUTOEXEC.BAT or TYPE DTP.BAT, depending on the name of the file you have written.

Fig. 1.6 A brief reminder of the Amstrad RPED editor program.

14 Desktop Publishing on a Shoestring

using the Fonts disk, because with this disk in place, there has to be space on the disk to keep a spare copy of the page you are working on (the file PUBLISH.WRK), and with this space reserved there is room for only four of the fonts. In addition, the disk that contains this spare copy file *must* be present at all times in Drive B. The size of the document that you are working on is limited by the amount of spare space on this disk. We need to look, then, at ways of rearranging the disks so that you can get more out of them.

```
        Volume in drive A has no label
        Directory of  A:\

        FONTMOVE EXE    53760   15-05-87   10:10
        FP       EXE   178160   22-06-87   17:00
        PRINTER  EXE    11142    5-04-87   18:09
        SNAP2ART EXE    15855    8-05-87   15:37
        SNAPSHOT COM     4145    8-05-87   15:38
        SETCOM1  BAT       24   11-05-87    9:59
        SETCOM2  BAT       24   11-05-87    9:59
        MASTER   DEF     5154   19-05-87   11:22
        SYSTEM   FNT     4714   28-02-86   13:37
        LASERDEF PS      5076   27-10-86   15:58
        SMOOTH   PS      5533   29-09-86   14:14
        UARTPAT2 PS      2425   10-07-86   13:20
        FSE      BAT       62   13-08-87   11:18
               13 File(s)      45056 bytes free
```

Fig. 1.7 The files on the original Fleet Street Editor System disk. Not all of these need to be present on your own start-up system disk.

The system disk, as it is copied from the original, contains the files shown in Figure 1.7. Now this leaves only about 45K on the disk, and most users of a twin-floppy machine will want to make a disk that will auto-load, meaning that you can put it into Drive A and switch on, or press Alt-Ctrl-Del, so that the operating system (MS-DOS) loads in and then the program starts running. When you format a disk with System tracks, however, you use some 70K of the disk space, so some changes have to be made. As it happens, not all of the files on the system disk are used in the form in which they come. The PRINTER.EXE program, for example is used to create a PRINT.DEF file for the printer you intend to use, and only the PRINT.DEF part is used. This allows you to create the file you need and delete the rest – but not from *this* copy! To make a more suitable System disk, follow the steps outlined below.

What Is Desktop Publishing? **15**

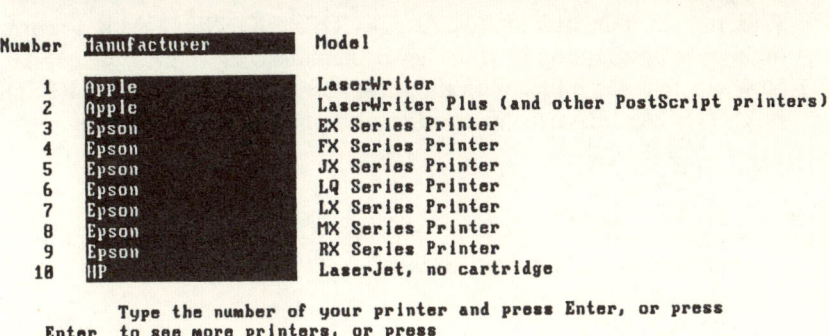

Fig. 1.8 The selection page of the PRINTER program. Using this program creates a file called PRINT.DEF on your disk/directory, and PRINTER need not be used again unless you change to another printer.

Users of 3.5. disks have considerably more disk space, but will still have to do some cutting and trimming along the same lines.

(1) Format two disks. Format one as an ordinary data disk, using FORMAT B: with the new disk in Drive B: and the MS-DOS disk in Drive A:. Format the other disk as a System disk, using FORMAT B:/S. Label this latter disk as SYSTEM to avoid any confusion.

(2) Copy the whole contents of your Fleet Street Editor System disk copy to the disk that has been formatted as a data disk (the unlabelled disk).

(3) Place this disk into Drive A. Type PRINTER (RETURN). You will see a display of printers, as indicated in Figure 1.8. Select your printer by typing its number and pressing RETURN (or press RETURN to search for the name of your printer). After selecting the printer, you are asked to specify the printer port. If you are using the normal parallel type of printer, this will be LPT1 for the Amstrad, selection 1.

(4) This creates a file PRINT.DEF on the disk. Now delete the files on this spare disk that are not needed in day-to-day use. The commands that you need are:

DEL PRINTER.EXE
DEL SNAP*.*
DEL *.BAT

– each followed by pressing RETURN.

(5) Now place this disk in Drive A and the disk that was formatted as a

16 *Desktop Publishing on a Shoestring*

System disk in Drive B:. Use COPY A:*.* B: to copy all the remaining files to B:.

(6) With the MS-DOS disk in drive A:, use COPY MOUSE.COM B: to copy the mouse program on to your new System disk.

(7) Now create a batch file. With the MS-DOS disk in drive A, use RPED B:AUTOEXEC.BAT to create a file, and put into it the following:

    echo off
    mouse
    cls
    echo Fleet Street Editor is loading
    fp

- then quit (Esc key, then F4).

(8) You should now have a disk whose directory looks as shown in Figure 1.9, but with MOUSE.COM also present. This disk can be placed into the A: drive and used to autoload when you switch on or reset the computer.

Note that when you start up Fleet Street Editor in this way you *must* have the Fonts disk copy in Drive B: also. You will be notified by a message on the screen if you forget this.

The Fonts disk

When you are working with a twin-floppy drive, the spare room on the Fonts

```
        Volume in drive A has no label
        Directory of  A:\

        COMMAND   COM      23612    7-14-86    12:13p
        FONTMOVE  EXE      53760    5-15-87    10:10a
        FP        EXE     178160    6-22-87     5:00p
        MASTER    DEF       5154    5-19-87    11:22a
        SYSTEM    FNT       4714    2-28-86     1:37p
        LASERDEF  PS        5076   10-27-86     3:58p
        SMOOTH    PS        5533    9-29-86     2:14p
        UARTPAT2  PS        2425    7-10-86     1:20p
        PRINT     DEF        147    7-26-88     3:34p
        AUTOEXEC  BAT         73    7-26-88     3:40p
               10 File(s)        31744 bytes free
```

Fig. 1.9 The directory of a suitable start-up system disk, to which MOUSE.COM needs to be copied from your MS-DOS disk. To run Fleet Street Editor from this disk, place in Drive A, then reset (press Alt-Ctrl-Del).

What Is Desktop Publishing? 17

disk determines how much space is available for your publications. Desktop publishing requires a lot of space, and Figure 1.10 shows that the standard Fonts disk leaves you only about 40K. This is despite the fact that your completed disk files will be put onto a data disk in the A: drive, and there can be around 300K of space free on that disk. The really free use of fonts is available only to the hard disk user (and is still subject to restrictions), but you need not be too inhibited by this use of the Fonts disk, because it's unlikely that the space on the Fonts disk will worry anyone who is truly a shoestring desktop publishing user.

```
Volume in drive A has no label
Directory of    A:\

FONTSLJ    DIC        81    17-04-87    12:59
FONTSLJB   DIC       560    23-05-86    15:35
FONTSLJF   DIC       588    12-05-87    13:14
FONTSLJP   DIC       185    12-05-87    13:24
FONTSLW    DIC       391    20-06-86     8:38
FP         OVL    135600    22-06-87    17:00
FONTSB     WID      1344     8-10-86    12:05
FONTSF     WID      3136     8-10-86    12:04
MASTER     FNT    170714    21-04-87    15:15
        9 File(s)          44032 bytes free
```

Fig. 1.10 The contents of the standard Fonts disk. This leaves the absolute minimum of room on the disk, so nothing must be added unless some of the contents can be deleted. You must always have this disk in Drive B of a twin-floppy machine.

Where the restriction becomes most irksome is when you want to use a greater variety of fonts than you have on the existing copy of the Fonts disk. If you find, for example, that you would like to add the Toronto font to use on your work, you will need to delete some other font, or at least parts of other fonts, from the Fonts disk in order to ensure that you have this minimum storage space of around 44000 bytes left. As it happens, the standard set of fonts on the Fonts disk is very well-chosen, and unless you suddenly develop marked likes and dislikes in font design there is really no need to change. You might find, however, that you have no need for the Courier font, because you never work with columns of tabular work. The Courier font is like typewriter print, each letter is allocated the same width so that it is easy to line up words under each other. If you do not have this requirement, however, you might feel that there was no point in having a font that looks rather like typed work, so that you could live without Courier, and substitute something else. Another possibility is that you might want to delete some of the italic styles in the larger sizes of type, because these are not so much used as the normal and bold.

The New York font on your Fonts disk is a particularly useful one; because it consists of a large range of sizes, nearly all of which exist in italic, normal and bold styles, and it's unlikely that you would want to dispense with this font, though you might delete some of the italic sets in the larger sizes. Before we get into details of how this is done, though, some guidance on the language of printing might be helpful at this juncture. The first word that you find turning up is *point*. The point is the unit of measurement for type, and one point is approximately $\frac{1}{72}$ inch. Type that is described as 10-point is therefore $\frac{10}{72}$" high – but what does that mean, since each letter is of different height? You might expect that this would be an average size, but it is, in fact, the size allowed for the highest letters, the capitals. Point sizes from 6 (very small) to 36 (headline) are used as a matter of course in printing, but the size that you can clearly see on the screen makes the use of 6 point rather, well, pointless. The New York font ranges from 9 point to 36 point, making it one of the most useful of the fonts that you have on your Fonts disk. Only the laser printer typeface POSTSCRIPT Times has a greater range (you can use this face even though it is a laser printer font, as Chapter 6 demonstrates), and is probably the best all-round typeface if you are interested in creating newsletters.

In each size of type you have normally the choice of three *styles*. These are 'italic', 'normal' and 'bold'. Italic is a slanting form of print which is often used to indicate quoted words, or to distinguish some piece of text from another. Normal is the style for the bulk of your material, and bold is used for headlines and sub-headings, and for the emphasis of a word or phrase. A few fonts (not the standard set) can offer bold-italic also. As is the case for all 'effects', the use of italic and bold has the maximum impact when you don't overdo it. Figure 1.11 shows the 14 point New York typeface in its italic, normal and bold styles, and you can see not only the different effects, but the letter spacings, and how the bold style letters require more room. A line of 9 point New York is included for comparison. A complete set of sizes and styles

This is New York 14-point normal
This is New York 14-point Bold
This is New York 14-point Italic
This is 9-point normal, not available in bold or italic

Fig. 1.11 Some examples of the New York font, showing styles and sizes.

constitutes a font when all the letters have been designed in the same way. This does not imply that each font that you can use for desktop publishing will contain every point size that you can use, and each of the three styles. Only a few fonts contain a really wide range, because there are many typefaces that are used only for bulk text, never for headlines or for footnotes, so that the extremes of size are never used. Such fonts might come in only a few sizes, some in one only. Some fonts are for specialised use and come in only one style and size, like Los Angeles. The fonts of Fleet Street Editor, incidentally, mostly carry the US names rather then the ones that will be more familiar to typesetters in the UK, so don't look for names like Baskerville or Monotype if you have been an Adana owner in times past.

There is quite a large range of fonts supplied with Fleet Street Editor, contained in the EXTRA.FNT file on the Sampler disk, and the manual for Fleet Street Editor shows what these fonts look like. If all this is not enough, you can buy disks of additional fonts, packaged as Executive Fonts and Decorative Fonts. Each package consists of two $5\frac{1}{4}''$ disks and one 3.5" disk containing a number of fonts. The Executive fonts are all in the larger sizes, and include one whopping 72 point in Quebec. The Decorative Fonts are for fancy work and are also in the larger sizes up to 72 point. You would therefore buy these extra fonts mainly for poster and similar work rather than for use with a newsletter, and their appearances are shown in Chapter 5. Note that you have one Font, Cairo, on the EXTRA.FNT set, which consists of miniature pictures only, and is used for decorative borders, underlines and similar purposes.

A New Fonts disk

Suppose that you are working with a twin-floppy machine and need to use a set of fonts drawn from EXTRA.FNT or other sources? The best way around this is to create a new Fonts disk for yourself, containing the alternative fonts that you want to use, while keeping the original copy of the fonts disk for everyday use. You need to decide what fonts you will want on the new disk, and where you will read them from, and you might at the same time decide to make some more space on your new Fonts disk so that you can have more than the minimum of 40K spare space on this disk.

Whether you are making more space or making a different font set, you need to use a program called FONTMOVE, which is on the System disk (the copy of the original, rather than the one that you have created for starting up the computer). The use of this program is not difficult, but unless you have some guidance (not given in the manual) you can spend rather a lot of time puzzling over what you should do next. The important point is that when you create a new Fonts disk, it must have at least two important files on it, one

20 *Desktop Publishing on a Shoestring*

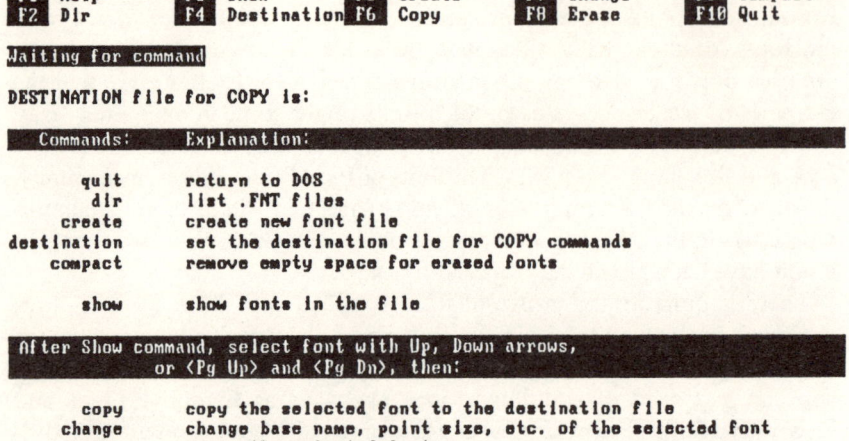

Fig. 1.12 The selection screen that the FONTMOVE program places before you. You will normally use F4 to make a destination of MASTER.FNT, and then F3 to type in the source file of fonts. When you are deleting fonts from MASTER.FNT, use F3 alone and type the name MASTER.FNT.

called FP.OVL, the other MASTER.FNT. Here are the steps for creating a new Fonts disk with a reduced number of fonts from the original master set.

(1) Make sure that you have a blank formatted disk handy. Create one if you have not (remember that you have to leave the program to carry out actions like disk formatting). Label this disk as FontMaster-2 or whatever name will remind you of what it contains.

(2) Place the copy of the *original* Fleet Street Editor System disk into Drive A, and the existing Fonts disk copy into drive B:. Type FONTMOVE (RETURN).

(3) When the action is complete and the title page of FONTMOVE appears, place the newly formatted disk in Drive B: and the existing Fonts disk in Drive A:.

(4) The FONTMASTER program shows the screen as in Figure 1.12. Pressing F2 (dir) gives a list of the files on the Fonts disk, so that you can see what is currently available.

(5) Press F5 to create a new font file, and specify when asked that it shall be B:MASTER.FNT. It is *very* important to put in the drive letter B: here.

(6) Now press F4 to show the destination for fonts, and type as the destination B:MASTER.FNT. This information will stay on the screen.

(7) Now press F3 to show the fonts. Figure 1.13 shows the appearance of the

```
Fontmove Program 1.0        Copyright (c) 1987 Software Publishing Corporation
 F1  Help          F3  Show         F5  Create      F7  Change      F9   Compact
 F2  Dir           F4  Destination  F6  Copy        F8  Erase       F10  Quit
Waiting for command

DESTINATION file for COPY is:       b:master.fnt

File shown below is:   master.fnt

Base Name:                 Point:       Style:              Printer:

Geneva                     14           Italic              Geneva
New York                    9           Normal              New York
New York                   10           Normal              New York
New York                   10           Italic              New York
New York                   12           Normal              New York
New York                   12           Bold                New York
New York                   14           Normal              New York
New York                   14           Bold                New York
New York                   14           Italic              New York
New York                   18           Normal              New York

       Use Up/Down arrows and <PgUp> <PgDn> to highlight correct font
```

Fig. 1.13 FONTMOVE in action. The selected part of the font is marked, so that this can be copied or deleted according to your choice. Do not delete any part of a font unless you have backup copies.

screen, which allows you to select a font by moving the cursor with the Up/Down arrows, and also with PgUp and PgDn. There are several pages on fonts, because each typeface is listed, showing each combination of size and style. You cannot copy all the members of a complete font in one action.

(8) For each font member that you want, place the cursor over it, press F6 to copy to the destination file of MASTER.FNT. Press F10 to quit when copying is completed.

As an example, I copied over a selection of fonts from the original MASTER.FNT disk, omitting Courier sizes and styles and also the italic faces in the larger New York sizes. The directory of the resulting disk is shown in Figure 1.14, showing that some 104000 bytes are now free on the disk. This could be useful if you find that you are having problems with restricted space on the original MASTER.FNT disk.

You could also, of course, copy from the EXTRA.FNT set. To do this, you follow the same steps, but with the Fleet Street Editor System disk copy in Drive A for step 4 onwards.

Hard disk users

As usual, users of a hard disk have the best of it. With the MASTER.FNT

```
Volume in drive A has no label
Directory of  A:\

FP        OVL    135600    6-22-87   5:00p
MASTER    FNT    121737    7-26-88   4:06p
        2 File(s)      104448 bytes free
```

Fig. 1.14 A Fonts disk on which several font styles and sizes have been removed, leaving space for new fonts.

present in the Fleet Street Editor directory, you can use FONTMOVE to add fonts from XTRA.FNT to MASTER.FNT as you wish. Since MASTER.FNT can contain only a limited number of fonts (it contains the fonts in a compressed form, and its indexing techniques can cope with a limited number), you might get a message to the effect that the MASTER.FNT file cannot be used if you have packed too much in. This is likely only if you have attempted to pack every font you can lay your hands on into MASTER.FNT. If you want to make use of a very large number of fonts, create one set called MASTER1.FNT and another called MASTER2.FNT and copy either to MASTER.FNT as needed, using COPY MASTER1.FNT MASTER.FNT, for example, if both are in the same directory. You might find it convenient to have another directory for spare fonts and to copy into MASTER.FNT in the main directory.

Chapter Two
Getting Started

Getting started is always the most difficult part of desktop publishing, particularly when you are getting to grips with an unfamiliar program. Though Fleet Street Editor makes things as easy as possible, the hardware causes restrictions that can be irksome at times, but which you have to get used to. Amstrad PC 1512 users, for example, must realise that the screen display they use will distort everything to some extent, making all the letters and the artwork look too high and slim, and with one screen showing only a quarter of a page. Some types of IBM clone, using the Hercules add-on card, will show half a screen at a time, and with the dimensions of letters and artwork correct. The majority of readers, however, who use IBM or compatible machines with the popular CGA graphics card will simply have to put up with the rather distorted view, which applies only to the screen – the paper output is always correct. For some operations it is helpful to put up a temporary measuring grille on to the screen, but that's something we'll look at later.

Cursor and selection

If you have ever used a word processor program, then much of the methods for typing text into Fleet Street Editor will be familiar to you. The position of a typed letter on the screen is indicated by a cursor, a thin vertical line. This cursor can be moved around text that has already been typed by using the keys marked with arrows, the PgUp and PgDn keys, and the Home and End keys. Other computer types will have keys that correspond to those. Moving up and down a page of typing can be done either with the PgUp and PgDn keys or, with better control by the 'elevator bar'. This is a vertical narrow box at the right hand side of the screen, which contains in turn a small square box. Moving this box will alter which part of a page of text you see on the screen. The box is most easily moved by placing the mouse pointer (the curly I) on the box, holding down the mouse button, and moving the mouse up or down (dragging the indicator bar). Releasing the mouse pointer will make the screen change to show the correct part of the page. You can also place the mouse cursor on part of the vertical track for the box and click the button to make the box move to this point, so making the screen change. The indicator bar can also be moved by placing the cursor over it, using the arrowed keys, then pressing the F10 key, moving the indicator with the keys marked with a vertical arrow, then pressing the F10 key again. An indicator bar type of display is also used in menus of files. If you are using an Amstrad PC type of machine, the use of indicator bars should be familiar to you and will be described in the part of the manual that deals with the Gem system.

The most important aspect of getting started is planning what you are going to print. In this book, the examples are necessarily short, and make use of a very restricted page width simply to allow for easy reproduction without having to reduce the images too much. For your own work you can expand out, but the maximum size of a single Fleet Street Editor page is about 8.5" × 10.5", with a printed area of about 8" × 10". This does not mean that you have to fill this page, and if you want to make master copies for posters, you can use several pages and copy each to a larger format if you have a copier of the appropriate size. Another option for creating posters is to print a copy on a normal size of page, and then use an enlarging copier to make the poster.

The first example we shall look at is one that uses text only, in the simplest way. We shall imagine that this is the start of the editorial in the local Philatelic Club newsletter, so that we shall have the title of the Club, the sub-title *Editor's Page*, and then the text. The layout will be as in Figure 2.1, with the main heading in large type, 24 point, the sub-heading smaller, 14 point, and the text in some normal size, perhaps either 10 point or 12 point. If the newsletter is printed on A5 paper, then it will have a printed area close to the limits that this book has required, but on A4 paper you could afford to spread out to a larger width.

Starting up Fleet Street Editor

Once you have some idea of what you want to do, start up Fleet Street Editor. With a twin-disk machine, place the Fonts disk in Drive B: and the System start-up disk in Drive A: and then switch on or reset the computer. When the program has loaded, take out the System start-up disk and put in a blank formatted disk, which will be your data disk. When your work on this example is complete, you will be able to record a file on this disk, using a name of your choice (but ending with *.PUB*) that will allow you to recall all of this page (or set of pages) and time you need to. You could also, if you liked, keep just the heading part as a .PUB file so that you never need to type it again.

The first thing you need to do is to check your page details. Every Fleet

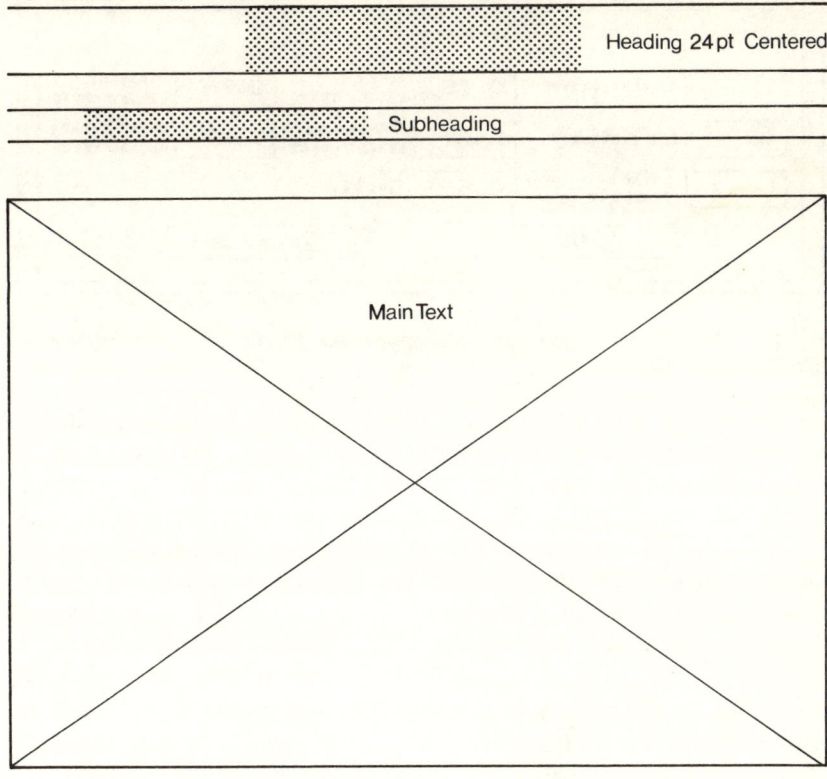

Fig. 2.1 The layout plan for a piece of text. This need not show much detail, only the proposed arrangement of text on the page.

Street Editor main action can be carried out by keys or mouse, and to check your page details you can either:

(1) move the mouse so that the mouse pointer (like a curly letter I) is over the Page heading, when the pointer becomes an arrow, then click (press and release) the mouse button; or
(2) press the F2 key.

Note that all actions that require keys show what these keys are. The main actions use the F-keys, others use the Alt-letter keys.

You should now select Define Page. Once again, this can be done with the mouse (move pointer to Define Page and click) or by pressing the down-arrow key and then RETURN. You should now see the display as indicated in Figure 2.2. This is the Define Page display, allowing you to specify what

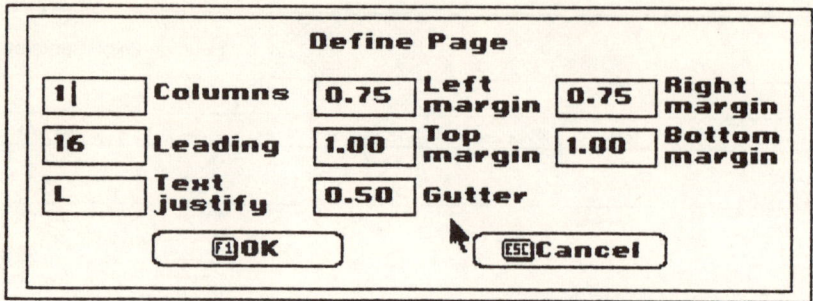

Fig. 2.2 The Define Page menu as it appears on the screen. The cursor is in the Columns box.

you want to use. Note that page width and depth is *not* mentioned, so that if you want a narrower or shallower page, or both, you do this by working on the margins. For this book, I was working with 2″ margins. The standard page is 8.5″ × 10.5″, and for illustrations I needed to keep to a maximum of 4.5″ width, so that I needed to use a 2″ margin each side. This is not something that you will have to do unless you are working to a limited page layout size, so there is no reason, if you have paper which is at least 8.5″ wide, why you should not stick to the sizes that are shown, with a 0.75″ margin each side.

What else do you need to do? When you are starting out in desktop publishing, the less you need to do the better, because it's only too easy to spend so much time in preparation that you never get anything done, and so never acquire the experience. We are using just one column, since this is a newsletter and not a newspaper, and this makes both the Columns and the Gutter entry of no particular interest. When you break your work into columns, newspaper style, you can use Columns to specify the number of columns in the page width (a limit of 3 is usual), and the Gutter is the space between columns. That's a topic that we shall look at later.

Meantime, the important items, once you have decided what margins you want, are Text justify and Leading. Text justify can be L, R or J, and refers to the positioning of the text in the line. Left justification, which is normal, means that the first letter in each line is placed on the left hand margin unless you have put in a space for a new paragraph. (C means centring, which is dealt with later.) Right justification, sometimes used for addresses, means that the lines are arranged to have the last letter hard against the right hand margin. Full justification (J) means that each line is of equal length, padded out with spaces to ensure that all the letters lie exactly between the margins, as indicated in Figure 2.3. Full justification can sometimes cause rather comic results, as this illustration shows, with one word at each margin, and when you opt for full justification you may have to carry out manual adjustments. There is no doubt, however, that the use of fully justified lines makes for very

This is left justified, with the first character
placed hard against the left margin.
                              This is right justified.
This is fully justified, with the text evenly placed
against both margins, with padding spaces used
wherever   necessary.

Fig. 2.3 Justification illustrated, showing the difference between left justification (the default), right justification, and full justification.

good-looking text which really distinguishes desktop publishing work from typed work. A good word processor will also carry out full justification, and will often be more sensible about lines which contain only a few words, but very few word processors can carry out full justification on lines in which the letters are proportionally spaced as distinct from using the same fixed space for each letter.

The safest option, as you will see later, is to leave the justification set at L. If you select J for full justification, you will get *everything* justified, including the heading and sub-heading. It is much better to opt for left justification at this point, and decide about individual lines and sets of lines later. The only remaining thing we have to think about now is leading, pronounced 'ledding' to rhyme with bedding. This refers to the spacing between lines, and the name comes from the way in which this used to be done, inserting strips of lead alloy between lines of type, with the edge of the lead alloy strip recessed so that it never touched the ink and so made no impression on the page.

Fleet Street Editor, always helpful, will generally set leading values for you so that you never have lines overlapping or looking ridiculously spaced out. You may, however, want to alter the leading when you take a critical look at your work, so that it's always better to set a value here. The value to set is the optimum leading for the *smallest* point size you use, because Fleet Street Editor will adjust upwards as needed and restore where needed, but adjustments to smaller than the value set here are not possible. How do you know what value to use? Leading is a matter of taste, but the Fleet Street Editor manual shows values that are accepted as being optimum for each of the fonts in the standard set. The table is in the Page Layout section in Chapter 3 (Functions) of the manual, and shows the leading for each size and style. The smallest face we shall be using in this example is New York 10 point, so that a leading of 12 is appropriate. Move the cursor to the Leading box, and type the figure of 12, then use the mouse to click on OK, or press F1 to acknowledge that you are finished with the Define Page menu. (As an example of leading in practice, the text of this book has been set in 10 point Times on 12 point leading, referred to as '10/12 point Times'.)

28 *Desktop Publishing on a Shoestring*

Typing the page

Once you have finished with your Define Page menu, you are presented with a screen which contains a set of menu items at the top, a set of symbols down the right hand side and one or two cursors. The text cursor is the thin vertical line, which will indicate where text will be typed. If you are not using a mouse, this will be the only cursor, but mouse users will see also the 'curly I' cursor which moves as you move the mouse and can be used for selecting items. Typing text into the page space is very similar to typing into a word processor, but with a very much greater range of choice. Like a word processor, Fleet Street Editor allows you to make corrections and amendments as you go along, or later, and you need never worry that what you are doing might require a lot of retyping at some later stage. The display down the right hand side of the screen allows you to pick various effects, the side tools, that can be selected and used with the mouse or by the F9 and arrowed keys. We'll look at these side tools later.

We want to use New York font, because of its versatility, and we'll start with the heading Philately Newsletter. This is to be in New York 24 point, and since it is a heading, it's best made bold. Place the mouse on Font and select New York by clicking (or use the F4 key, then down arrow and RETURN). With the font selected, move the mouse to Style (or F5). In this menu you can first select the size, 24 point, and then the style, bold. Note that this requires you to make the selection action twice. Selections that *cannot* be made are in light grey letters, and for some combinations of style and size you might have to pick style before size, for others size before style. Check with another look at the menu that you have selected both 24 point and bold, Figure 2.4. Moving the mouse away from the selection box will remove the box from view.

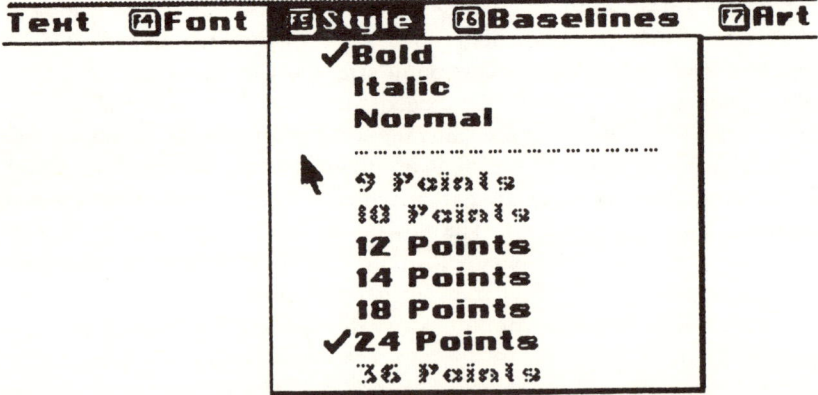

Fig. 2.4 Checking the style and size of print.

With this font selection made, you can now type the heading, Philately Newsletter. If you are a good touch-typist then it's possible that you could type too fast for Fleet Street Editor to keep up with, because forming the letters on the screen, using the correct font and size, can take longer than just placing a standard letter, as a word processor does. If you find that you are beating the program for speed, you will just have to slow down. Most of us will not suffer from this problem, certainly not when we first start using Fleet Street Editor, but when you start to use some of the fancier fonts in the larger sizes you might find that your typing speed has to be reduced.

Having typed the headline, press RETURN to take a new line. This will consist of Editor's Page, and for this we want the 14 point Normal face of New York font. Select Style again, and pick 14 point and Normal, checking once again before you start to type that both these items have been selected, as indicated by the ticks. Remember that the screen images are elongated on the Amstrad PC and on many other PC compatibles. You can now type the Editor's Page line, and press RETURN at the end. Press RETURN again to create an extra space between this and the text.

Now select the third face, using the Style menu to get 12 point and normal. With this you can start the newsletter in earnest – I have typed just a few lines. When you are starting with Fleet Street Editor, it's better to keep to single page work at the start, because this avoids a lot of complications as well as a lot of effort. If you have existing text in the form of a word processor file, of course, you might like to load this in without typing – but that's a more advanced topic for later.

With your text typed, you might wonder how you are supposed to make reasoned judgements on text and layout when everything is tall and slim, like a Cinemascope film projected with the wrong lens. One answer is to use page preview. If you select Page and then Show Page, you will see a miniature version of your page, with no detail, but with everything in perfect proportion. This can be very helpful later when you are adjusting things, but for the moment just take a look and then return to normal (click the mouse anywhere else).

Now print your page. Select File, then Print. You will see the selection as indicated in Figure 2.5, and normally the only thing you will want to alter here is the standard of printing. For a quick look at what you have composed, select Draft – this is selected for you by default in any case when you first use the Print command. Make sure that there is paper in the printer, either continuous or single sheet. If you are using single sheets, set the printer so that the end-of-paper switch is disabled. If you do not do this, then the printer will stop before the paper has been rolled out, and will beep at you to insert more paper. This problem does not arise if you are using continuous paper, but for desktop publishing work it's more usual to have single sheets, because this allows you to use high-quality glossy paper for your final print.

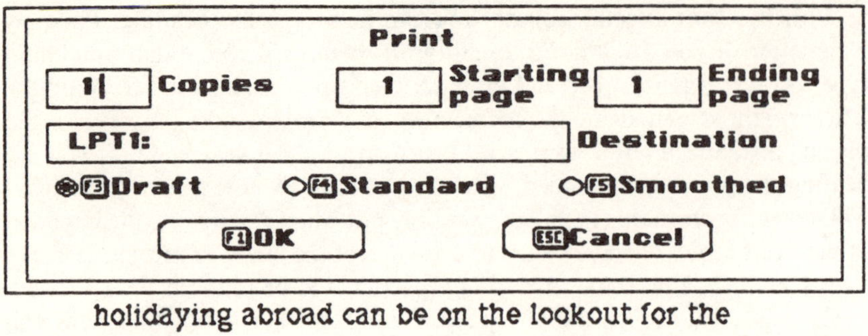

```
           Print
┌──┐        ┌─┐ Starting  ┌─┐ Ending
│1 │ Copies │1│ page      │1│ page
└──┘        └─┘           └─┘
┌─────────────────────────────────────┐
│ LPT1:                    Destination│
└─────────────────────────────────────┘
 ⊙[F3]Draft   ○[F4]Standard   ○[F5]Smoothed

      [[F1]OK]          [[ESC]Cancel]
```

holidaying abroad can be on the lookout for the

Fig. 2.5 The Print selection box. This automatically selects a draft print for you first time round.

For a final effort you can use Standard or Smoothed. The Smoothed gives really excellent results on a dot-matrix printer, and is to be preferred unless you are using very small typefaces (which can look rather over-black when Smoothed is used). Figure 2.6 is a smoothed printout of the example – but you should not print one for yourself yet. The draft version is good enough for the moment, because what we need to look at now is how to adjust this work so that it looks better. This is something that you will later do on-screen, though you will probably always want to make a draft copy simply for final checking and in order to keep a copy of your work.

At this point also, you should save your work. Select File, then Save. You will be presented with a selection box, into which you can type a filename of up to eight letters, like MYFIRST or NEWSLET1. The default extension is .PUB, meaning a complete publication – make sure that this has been selected as in Figure 2.7. The .MAC extension is for collections of artwork only, and

Philately Newsletter
Editor's Page

Hello again, readers in August. During this time of summer holidays, you probably have had very little thought of working with your collections. This is a time, however, when those of you who are holidaying abroad can be on the lookout for the unusual in the way of stamps.

Fig. 2.6 The example of newsletter printed with Smoothed mode.

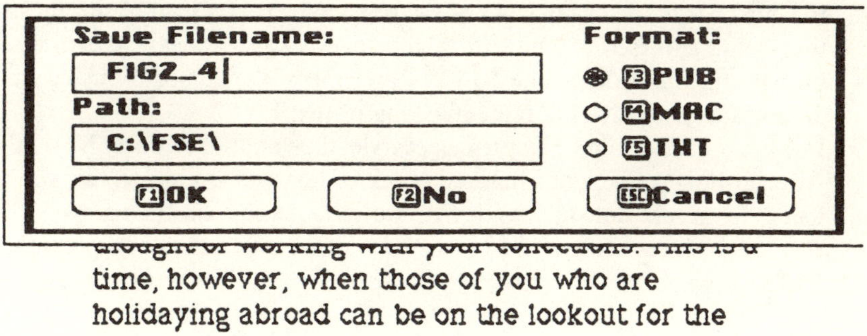

```
┌─────────────────────────────────────────────────────────┐
│  Save Filename:              Format:                    │
│  ┌──────────────┐                                       │
│  │ FIG2_4│      │             ● F3 PUB                  │
│  └──────────────┘                                       │
│  Path:                       ○ F4 MAC                   │
│  ┌──────────────┐                                       │
│  │ C:\FSE\      │             ○ F5 TXT                  │
│  └──────────────┘                                       │
│  ( F1 OK )      ( F2 No )        ( ESC Cancel )         │
└─────────────────────────────────────────────────────────┘
```

time, however, when those of you who are
holidaying abroad can be on the lookout for the

Fig. 2.7 The SAVE selection box. The default extension is PUB, and this is the one that you are most likely to use.

.TXT is for recording text only in standard form that can be read by a word processor, with no font or style information. If you forget to type a name, the name NEW will be used, and you will have to delete this name (using the backspace/delete left key) before you enter a new name. Press RETURN when you have typed the name, omitting the .PUB extension.

A few alterations

Take a critical look at the example in Figure 2.6. To start with, it would be better to have the main heading centred. Make a note of this. The sub-heading looks rather too close to the main headline. Would you want the sub-heading centred, or would it look better if it were just indented slightly? Is the double space between Editor's Page and the first line just a little too great, and would it be better to indent the first word of the text, as you would indent each first word of a new paragraph. Is the choice of 12 point for the main text suitable, and would 10 point, fully justified, look better? These are details of appearance that distinguish typography from just typesetting, and they are the value judgements that you learn by experience and by training your eyes rather than by following rules. At this point, then, we need to find out how to make alterations, starting with the comparatively simple topic of changing style and size (or font if need be).

The change that we shall make is to the main body of the text, whose letters look rather too large for the purpose. The existing size is 12 point, and we shall change this to 10 point. A change like this to a block of text is carried out by marking the block of text and then using the appropriate menu. In this case, the menu to use is the Style menu which contains the sizes.

(1) Place the text cursor at the start of the block, which can be on the first letter of the main body of text.
(2) Press down the mouse button, hold it down, and move the mouse so that

the cursor is moved to the end of the block of text. This will result in the text being reversed – white on black in this case. Release the mouse button. (*Or* hold down the F10 key and move the cursor by using the arrowed keys to give the same marking of text.)
(3) Use the mouse or the F5 key to select style, then choose 10 point Normal. After a short pause, your marked block of text will change to this size.
(4) Click the mouse button outside the marked area to clear the marking. If you are mouseless, move the cursor with the arrowed keys and press the F10 key twice.

The result of all this, a process which very quickly becomes familiar and easy, is to change the text to 10 point. All changes in style and size, or even complete fonts, are made in this way. For text that you are about to type, you can select a font, size of style which will be used from that point until you make another font, size or style selection. You can also delete, move and copy blocks of text in a way that is almost identical to the methods used in most word processors.

The change of size is accomplished by marking the text as described, and in fact, all changes require some kind of marking to show the extent of the change. Other types of change, however, including the spacing of text in the line and the spacing between lines (leading) require a different form of marking which is brought about by using the *Baselines* menu. We shall make a start on this kind of marking by centring the main heading of this example.

(1) Place the cursor at the start of the main heading, Philately Newsletter.
(2) Select the Baselines menu (mouse or F6) and then *Adjust single* (mouse or Alt-A).
(3) Select the top line again by clicking the mouse anywhere on the text or by using the F10 key with the cursor on the text. The marking that appears shows lines under each line of text, with the selected line marked with three small black squares (called 'handles'), one at each end and one in the middle. Note that the text is no longer readable at this point. In some of these actions, the text will disappear, but it will be restored later.
(4) Select Baselines, again, and then *Center*.
(5) Select Baselines again, and select Adjust single again. Adjust single, like several menu choices, has a *toggle* action, meaning that you select it once to turn it on, and select again to turn it off.

After this last operation, you should see the heading centred over the page width that you are using (remember that these illustrations are printed with a deliberately restricted page width in order to fit this book size). The spelling 'Center' reminds you that Fleet Street Editor is of US origin (perhaps it should be New York Editor), and you will see other reminders of its origin as you make more use of the program.

Now you can make a few minor adjustments, using ordinary editing methods. Place the cursor at the first letter of the sub-heading, the E of Editor's, and use the space-bar to move this phrase over. Try placing it under the P of Philately. You can also indent (move over to the right) the start of the main text. As a start, try moving it about half as much as you moved the sub-heading of Editor's Page.

Now we can look at how the main body of text can be fully justified. This is done *after* any indenting, otherwise the indenting would upset the justification. If you feel that some lines are too short for full justification, you can bring back a word from the next line and hyphenate it, or if the short line is the last in a paragraph, you can leave it unjustified. This is going rather too far for the moment, however, and we want to look at how straightforward full justification is carried out, because in this example there are no spacing problems.

(1) Place the cursor at the start of the text – on the left hand margin of the first line (not on the first letter).
(2) Mark with Baselines. Select Baselines and then *Adjust below*, because you want to justify all of this column from this line down.
(3) Mark the first line in the column of main text, using the mouse or using the arrowed keys and F10. Baseline marking depends on the cursor being on the text of the line, and you don't always succeed first time round until you get used to positioning the cursor correctly.
(4) Select Baselines again, then *Full justify*.
(5) Select Baselines again and then *Adjust column* again to end the action.

You will now find that your main 10 point text is fully justified, and the justification looks well done, with no excessive spaces.

The page still looks rather unsatisfactory, though, mainly because of the spacing between the headings. The headings are too close, and the main text is too far from the sub-heading. Start adjusting this by deleting one space by placing the cursor on the left hand margin (not the first letter) of the main text, and then pressing the Del key (note that the Amstrad Del left key does not work in Fleet Street Editor). This places the main text closer to the sub-heading, and when you make a draft print you will probably feel that it is now too close. This calls for baseline adjustments.

As before, the Baselines menu has to be used. When the baselines appear, you can make adjustments in both baseline length (not required here) or in spacing. The spacing changes are made by placing the cursor on the central 'handle' of the baseline, and moving up or down, using the mouse (button held down) or by pressing the F10 key, using the arrowed keys and then pressing the F10 key again. You can select to use adjust above or adjust below. If you select adjust above, then the Baseline with the handles and all baselines above it will be affected. If you select adjust below, then the marked baseline and all below it will be affected. Selecting Adjust column will affect all baselines, the marked line and all above and below. The other option, the one we have used so far, is Adjust single.

Now this is all very well, and you can play for hours adjusting spacings in this way, but it's not very reproducible. Once you have created a layout that you like, how would you make another one with different lettering? One answer, of course, is to edit this one, but if you make changes to the Page Definition, then your alterations will be lost. There is another way of changing the spacings, which is to use the Adjust leading option in the Baselines menu.

(1) Place the cursor on the Editor's Page line, and mark, using *Baselines* and *Adjust single*.
(2) Choose *Change leading*. A notice will show what leading is presently in use between this line and the line above. Alter this to a smaller figure, 22 in this example. Restore to the normal image and look at the result.
(3) Repeat, selecting the first line of main text, and this time making the leading greater (I used 16). Restore the normal image.
(4) You may find that some of the text looks less readable, notably the last line of text. Select the Realign Text option of the Baselines menu to correct this.

Now you can print another draft copy, and decide on any other changes you might want. The importance of using leading for separating is that you can take a note of the leading numbers on your draft copy, making it easier to select this again. The state of your leading can be found at any time when you are editing by pressing the Ctrl-F1 keys. This brings the Status Box on to the screen, informing you of the printer you are using, the font, size and style, the leading and the number of visible characters, together with any characters that have overflowed from the page and which can be copied to the Clipboard and so to another page (see later). Keeping track like this is much more difficult when you have used baseline movement by way of the mouse or arrowed keys. The result of all this work on the Philately Newsletter is shown in Figure 2.8. This might not be entirely pleasing to a professional typographer, but it's a world away from the Newsletter which used typed copy and the old duplicator. You might, perhaps, want a little more leading in the main text – but you can't spend all your time making fine adjustments. Perhaps on the next issue...

The important point is that all the work you put into something like this need not be repeated. Unless your newsletter changes its name, or ceases to have an Editor's Page, then this layout can be stored. Once this issue has been copied and distributed, you can recall the file, delete the main text (or leave the first line as a guide), and save again, changing the name to something like EDTEMP.PUB to remind you that this is the template for the Editor's page.

Philately Newsletter
Editor's Page

Hello again, readers in August. During this time of summer holidays, you probably have had very little thought of working with your collections. This is a time, however, when those of you who are holidaying abroad can be on the lookout for the unusual in the way of stamps.

Fig. 2.8 The latest version of the newsletter example.

Next time you have to write an Editor's Page, you recall this template, type in your new text (deleting any text you left in), check that the leading looks right, and print it out. All these actions of baseline adjustment need not be repeated, though you still have to use the Baselines menu to carry out the justification of the lines of text.

Hyphenation and justification

The example we have been working with so far has presented no justification problems, and a lot of text, particularly if you keep to short words, will never present problems. Trouble starts when you have a long word at the end of a line which gets carried on to the next line, leaving a gap, so that the action of full justification rearranges the words in the line. This type of problem affects short lines particularly, and is a continual worry if you are dealing with newspaper columns of, typically, only 30 characters per line. The answer is to hyphenate long words which would otherwise be taken on to the next line, leaving a gap. Some word processors, and some desktop publishing programs can do this automatically, which does not necessarily mean that it is done as you would want it. Fleet Street Editor has no provision for automatic hyphenation.

Take a look at Figure 2.9, which illustrates what I mean. The short paragraph in (a) has used the word 'typographical', which is taken over to the next line as you type it. Structural is also treated in the same way. Now you could have inserted hyphenation at the time of typing, deleting back as soon as you saw the part-word 'typogr' move to the next line. You could then type typo- and space until the next line was take, and then continue with the remainder of the word. It's more likely, however, that you will be concentrating on the typing rather than the line appearance at this point.

In example (b), the line length has been increased very slightly, because this allows the whole of the word 'Structural' to be brought back. At the same

(a) This is printed in Geneva 12-point, the default typographical choice of Fleet Street Editor. Structural changes are needed!

(b) This is printed in Geneva 12-point, the default typo- graphical choice of Fleet Street Editor. Structural changes are needed!

(c) This is printed in Geneva 12-point, the default typo- graphical choice of Fleet Street Editor.   Structural changes are needed!

Fig. 2.9 Carrying out hyphenation. This is not an automatic action, and you have to judge for yourself where you will want to use hyphens. Always do this when full justification is *not* in use – the text should be fully justified only after the hyphenation has been done.

time, 'typographical' has been split. This has been done by inserting the hyphen, and then a space, making the word into 'typo- graphical', and then placing the cursor on to the first letter and deleting backwards, so that the 'typo-' part moves to the line above. You will have to make sure that there is a space between the words 'default' and 'typo-'. If you dislike having to use the delete key for this purpose, you can use the Baselines menu along with *Realign text* to move typo- back into place (use Adjust above and place the handles on the third line). If you have a lot of such changes to carry out, the use of Realign text is much easier, but you still have to check back to make sure that the changes have been carried out as you would want them.

Once the lines have been adjusted, with hyphenation inserted in this way, you can apply full justification. This is done, as usual, by selecting baselines, then Adjust below, placing the handled line on to the first line of the example, and then selecting full justification. This, however, will make the words in the last line space out badly, in an ugly way. You can adjust this by using Baselines again, selecting Adjust single, and then left justification. The result of it all is shown in Figure 2.9(c). Even this would offend some typographers, who feel that the hyphen should not count as part of a line, and would take the word 'Structural' left by one space or place 'typo-' one space to the right. This is, as so often happens, a matter of taste, and it's *your* taste that counts.

Imported text

One way of taking out the weariness from hyphenation is to import text from a word processor program that hyphenates automatically. There are other reasons also for wanting to use word processed text. One very persuasive reason is that you are editing a newsletter to which several other people contribute, and they send you their work on disk, having used their own word processors. The V.3.0 version of Fleet Street Editor can cope with all of the main word processors whose text files are not a simple set of number codes (ASCII code, where the letters mean American Standard Code for Information Interchange). Users of Fleet Street Editor V.2.0 will have to insist that such contributions are changed into ASCII text. This is a facility that every word processor has (there are probably some that don't, but you are unlikely to find any used with either PC or PCW Amstrad machines). The other good reason is that you may want to type text very fast and make a spelling check. Fleet Street Editor does not permit very fast typing (although if you use a straightforward font it can keep up with all but the fastest typing), but spelling checking is very definitely a province of a good word processor. Users of Editor Plus on the Amstrad PCW machines can import their LocoScript files into Fleet Street Editor Plus after spell-checking by LocoSpell.

Given, then, that the use of a word processor along with Fleet Street Editor makes sense if you already have a word processor or receive word processed text on disk, the next step is to see how such text can be put into your published work. I shall use here as an example part of the first draft of the preface to this book, which was prepared on WordStar Professional 4. This text is not in ASCII form, but V.3.0 of Fleet Street Editor can read it with no problems. Users of V.2.0 of Fleet Street Editor will have to have the text converted to ASCII by the user of WordStar. Some versions contain conversion routines, and you can get programs that convert WordStar output into ASCII code (one such program is called simply F, and is a public domain program, meaning that you can get a copy for only the price of copying the disk). When you use automatic hyphenation with WordStar, however, conversion programs may remove the hyphens, so that some trial and error is needed before you can be sure of getting what you want. Users of V.3.0 of Fleet Street Editor, however, will have no problems since text files from all the major word processing programs (and that means also most of the lesser known ones) can be read with no conversion problems.

Let's suppose, then, that we have a file called, for the sake of example, IMPORT.TXT. The TXT extension to the name is *very* important, since without this, Fleet Street Editor will not recognise that the file is a text file for reading. If the file is called, for example, IMPORT.DOC or IMPORT.ASC or with any other extension then you will have to rename it. To load in this file:

(1) Start up Fleet Street Editor, and use Define Page to set your page size and layout.
(2) Select Text, and then Get text. If the file that you want to read is not on

the drive/disk/directory that you are currently using, you will not see it listed, and if no files with the .TXT extension exist on the drive/disk/directory you are using, you will get the notice shown in Figure 2.10.

(3) If necessary, use the Del keys to type in the correct route to the file. This affects hard disk users in particular, and in the example of Figure 2.10, I had to change the Path to C:\WSTAR\BOOKS\DTP to get the correct file. If you are using a twin-floppy machine, then you probably need only insert the disk containing the TXT file into Drive A. Remember that Drive B *must* always contain the Fonts disk.

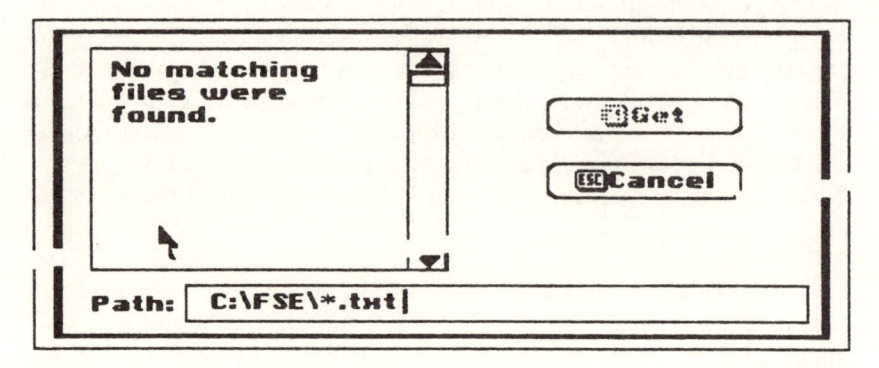

```
┌─────────────────────────────────────────────────┐
│  No matching       ▲                            │
│  files were          ┌──────────┐               │
│  found.              │  ⌂Get    │               │
│                      └──────────┘               │
│                      ┌──────────┐               │
│                      │[ESC]Cancel│               │
│                      └──────────┘               │
│      ▶                                          │
│                    ▼                            │
│  Path: │ C:\FSE\*.txt│                          │
└─────────────────────────────────────────────────┘
```

Fig. 2.10 A Matching File notice which in this case invites you to delete the Path shown and type in one that is more suitable.

(4) Once the TXT file is available, it will be read. Reading may take some time, particularly if the file requires more than one page.
(5) Check the file when it has been entered. Remember that Fleet Street Editor does not act like a word processor. It deals with one page at a time, and to get from one page to another you have to use the Page menu, selecting the Jump to Page option.

Once the text has been read, you can get to work on it. If you are using the same margins as the original text, the hyphens that exist to split up words in the original text will be correctly placed. If the imported text used different margins, however, there will be widespread chaos, with hyphens appearing in words that are not split. This can be avoided by adopting two simple rules:

(1) If you prepare your own text on a word processor, use a line length that is the same as you will set your page to with Define Page.
(2) If you take text from anyone else on disk, ask for ASCII text with no justification and no hyphens. This can save an enormous amount of effort.

You can then set to work on the text. A lot of imported text can be used with very little change, but one thing you have to watch is the use of a pound

Getting Started **39**

sign. A disk containing ASCII coded text will have no pound signs before numbers, because there is no standard ASCII code for the English pound (ASCII is an American code, remember). You have a pound key on the Amstrad, and Fleet Street Editor will show this on screen and print it for fonts that contain the pound. You will have to insert this symbol into your imported text, however, taking care that you insert it into the correct place.

> Desk Top Publishing is by this time well established, and there are many packages and books for the large- scale user who has no qualms at spending sums of the order of £7000 on equipment, and several hundred pounds per month on running costs. For each user in that category, however, there are ten whose means and requirements are considerably more modest. Items as diverse as the Church Newsletter, the Bob-a-job week leaflets, the menu for the small cafe or the hand-out advertising sheet for the ironmongers ; all are candidates for Desk Top Publishing techiques, but not at the prices that are associated with Laser Printers and expensive computers. It is to this majority group of users who need low-cost desk top publishing that this book is addressed.

Fig. 2.11 The start of a piece of imported text.

Figure 2.11 shows the first part of the imported preface from the text of this book. This has been converted, read into Fleet Street Editor V.2.0, and the pound sign inserted. The spacing has been cleaned up (the last line has been justified left) and then the extract printed. Note that when an imported file consists of more than one page, you are advised by a notice on the screen which page number is being read. A lot of shoestring desktop publishing work is single page work, and even for a newsletter it is possible to work with a separate file for each page, an approach that can make editing much simpler because you can be certain that nothing you do will then affect the whole of the Newsletter. If you enter text directly and come to the end of a page, the text entered from that point is held in the memory (the overflow area) until you specify a new page number and use the Move Text into Clipboard command.

You can then Paste the text into the new page, using the Paste command which will now be described.

Cut, Paste, Copy

Though Fleet Street Editor does not have the facilities of a full-blown word processor, it does have the Cut, Copy and Paste facilities that are shared by word processors. These actions apply to a block of text that has been marked either with the mouse or with the F10 and arrowed keys as described earlier. Using Cut on a marked block will remove that block into a memory area called the Clipboard, and subsequently using Paste will put the same block in at the position of the cursor. You can therefore shift a block of text from one position in a page to another (including another page) by marking, using cut, moving the cursor to the new position, and then using Paste. If you want to copy the text rather than moving it, then you mark it, use Copy, then move the cursor and use Paste. If the piece of text that you want to mark extends over the bottom of the screen, then you will have to mark using the F10 and arrow keys rather then with the mouse.

The use of Copy, Cut and Paste applies mainly when you type your work directly into Fleet Street Editor, or when you want to edit work that you have imported from a disk sent to you by someone else. If you prepare your own text on your own word processor, you will have done all the cutting, copying and pasting with the word processor and will not need to do any more with Fleet Street Editor. This is particularly important if you use V.2.0 of Fleet Street Editor, which is rather slow about these actions. For work done on a single page, however, which is what I advise until you have a really good knowledge of Fleet Street Editor, the Cut, Copy and Paste actions are fast enough, even on V.2.0, not to hold up your efforts.

Figure 2.12 shows these actions. The paragraph in (a) is simply used to show the position of the sentences. We can copy this paragraph twice as follows:

(1) Using either the mouse or the F10 and arrow keys, mark the whole of the paragraph.
(2) Select Text, and then Copy.
(3) Move the cursor to where you want to place the copy. Remember that you have to use the RETURN key to move the cursor to a new line which has not yet been used.
(4) Select Test, then Paste. This will put in the copy starting at the cursor position.

You can then make another copy, but this does *not* mean going over the whole procedure again. Once Cut or Copy has been used, the text is held in

(a) This would be better placed as the second sentence in this paragraph. Here is a sentence which we can use as the first in the paragraph. Finally, this is the last sentence.

(b) This would be better placed as the second sentence in this paragraph. *Here is a sentence which we can use as the first in the paragraph.* Finally, this is the last sentence.

(c) Here is a sentence which we can use as the first in the paragraph. This would be better placed as the second sentence in this paragraph. Finally, this is the last sentence.

Fig. 2.12 Using Cut and Paste. (a) The original text. (b) A sentence marked using the mouse. Selecting Cut will now make this sentence disappear, with the text rearranging itself. (c) The cut text pasted at the start. The cursor is placed at the start, and then Paste selected.

memory, and you can Paste it into different places as often as you like. Only one piece of text can ever be held at any one time, however, and if you use Cut or Copy again on another piece of text, then the first piece that you Cut or Copied will be lost.

You can now work on this copy.

(1) Place the cursor at the start of the second sentence, and mark the sentence. You can do this using the mouse (dragging the mouse) or with the F10 and arrowed keys. The effect is to mark the sentence by inverting the colour of the letters. In the illustration of Figure 2.12(b), this is indicated by shading.
(2) Select Text and Cut. This will remove the marked portion.
(3) Place the cursor at the start of the paragraph, and then select Text and Paste. This will place the Cut portion into the start of the text, as Figure 2.12(c) shows.

Copy can be useful if you have pages with headers and footers. A header is a word or phrase that appears at the top of each page, and a footer is another word or phrase that appears at the foot. Very often, for example, a book or magazine title appears as a header, and a page number as a footer.

If you are working on a document of several pages, you might want to have these headers and footers on each page, and the simplest method is to type them into the first page and then copy to the other pages. If the footer contains a page number, of course, you will need to alter this number for each page.

Once again, if you prepare your text on a word processor, this work could be done for you. Practically all word processors will put headers and footers automatically into text when it is printed, and it is also possible to make the word processor 'print' to a disk file instead of to paper. This disk file will usually be an ASCII file (if not, then it can be converted) and so can be read into Fleet Street Editor. Since it is a file representation of what would be printed, rather than just the disk file of text (in which the header and footer would appear once only, possibly not at all if it were removed by the conversion into ASCII code), there will be a header and footer for each page. If the word processor pages correspond exactly to your Fleet Street Editor pages, then the headers and footers will be in the correct places. If you do not have this much (abnormal) luck, then at least the headers and footers still exist, and you can move them into the correct positions by using Cut and Paste.

Cut, Copy and Paste techniques can be used with graphical images as well as with text, which is something that we shall be looking at in Chapter 4. In addition, we need to look at the possibilities of treating text as if it were artwork, which allows a lot of interesting, decorative and sometimes useful effects to be achieved. The next topic, however, is the use of columns, newspaper style, something that word processors can achieve only with difficulty but which Fleet Street Editor accomplishes with ease.

Chapter Three
More Text Techniques

A letterhead

One very useful application of desktop publishing is to create your own letterheads. These can include graphics shapes or pictures, but for the moment we'll look at text work only. Some ornamental work is permissible in a letterhead, using font types that would not normally be employed for larger amounts of text such as notices and newsletters, and this also is one of the applications for right justification. Figure 3.1 shows an example.

Figure 3.1 has been printed with a font that is not one of your normal set, 12 point Chicago bold. This font exists only in 12 point bold on your disk, and is one of the fonts on the EXTRA.FNT set on the Examples disk. To make use of it, I used FONTMOVE, making MASTER.FNT the destination and EXTRA.FNT the *Show* font set, moving this and a few other fonts, including Cairo. If you use twin floppies, then you can move a font in only when you move some fonts, or portions of fonts, out. If you have followed the pattern illustrated in Chapter 1, removing Courier (possibly retaining Courier 10 and 12 point normal) and also the larger italic styles, there should be room on your Fonts disk for the Chicago and for Cairo, possibly a few more. This allows you more variety without cramping your style too much. We shall be making use of Courier later in this chapter, so leave at least the 10 and 12 point normal Courier styles.

John F. Candida,
The Molehill,
Glemsbury,
Silts. ST11B 4TT

Fig. 3.1 An address typed using right justification, and intended to be used as a letterhead. The typeface is Chicago Bold 12 point.

To make the letterhead, the Page menu has been used to select Define Page, and the justification has been changed to R. The margin at the top of the page has been changed to 0.5″ (the smallest possible), though this would not be important unless you wanted to print each letterhead directly for yourself, a very time-consuming task. It would be more normal for you to produce a copy exactly as you want it, and then take this to a printer to be placed on several hundreds or thousands of sheets by offset litho. Of course, if you need only a dozen of so then print them directly by all means, but for large orders you need to use something rather less time-consuming.

Now when you opt for right-justification in the Define Page menu, the results can be slightly surprising when you start to type. The cursor starts over at the left hand side, in its usual place. When you press the first key, however, the letter appears on the right hand edge, along with the cursor, and then moves left as you type another letter. This can be particularly tricky when you type a space, because the *space does not appear* until you type another letter. This can give you the impression that you have not typed the space and lead to you putting in too many spaces. If you do, then you can edit them out by using the delete keys later. This type of name and address can, of course, be done in a variety of fonts, perhaps using one font for the name and another for the address, and fancy fonts can be used to your heart's content – but please remember that someone has to read it!

As an example of the use of the more decorative fonts, take a look at Figure 3.2. This has made use of the Cairo font – which comes only in normal (if you can call it normal) 18 point, the London font – which gives the grotesque gothic letters, and the Helvetica. Whether you like the result or not, it's a splendid exercise in the use of fonts, and also in the way that spacing can be juggled with, using Fleet Street Editor. It's when we try something of this sort that we realise that there are things that the manuals are not very helpful about.

👁👁👁👁👁👁👁👁👁👁👁👁👁
👁   𝔓𝔯𝔦𝔳𝔞𝔱𝔢 𝔈𝔶𝔢 𝔖𝔢𝔯𝔳𝔦𝔠𝔢𝔰   👁
👁👁 Richard Roughly-Going 👁👁
👁👁   Investigator   👁👁
👁👁👁👁👁👁👁👁👁👁👁👁👁

Fig. 3.2 A fancy heading, using Cairo font to produce the eyes, along with the London decorative font and Helvetica. The typing is simple, the spacing is not!

When you switch to a font and style combination, Fleet Street Editor will continue using that set of font, size and style until you change to something else. For example, if you are in 18 point Helvetica, and you type a name such as John, then three spaces, then change to 10 point New York to type Jones, how will this look? The answer is that you have John in 18 point, then three spaces of 18 point size, then Jones in 10 point. Now suppose you decide to delete a space or two in order to place the names closer to each other. You can certainly do this, but the movement for each delete step is the size of an 18 point space, and if you put in extra spaces with the spacebar, then each space is of 18 point size.

Now suppose that you had approached this differently. You select 18 point Helvetica, and type the name John as before, but you then change to 10 point New York. You then type as many spaces as you want, then the name Jones. Because the spaces are now 10 point spaces, you can adjust the distance between the names in much finer steps now, 10 point steps. Finally, if you type John in 18 point Helvetica, then select 10 point New York and type ten spaces, then select 18 point Helvetica and type Jones, you will find that you can adjust the distance between the name in small 10 point steps, but the names remain in large type.

This arrangement by which a font remains in use until the next font is selected can cause considerable bewilderment until you have had some experience of it, and particularly when you are making alterations to a piece of work. You might, for example, want to add something to a line of text, using a smaller font. Perhaps you have a name in 14 point, and you want to add MIEE in 10 point capitals following the name. The important point is where you have the cursor when you select the 10 point. If the cursor is not at the place where you intend to type MIEE, then when you put the cursor into this place, your selection will *automatically* have changed back to the 14 point size. The correct procedure is to place the cursor where you want to place the letters, then change font/size/style, then type. For almost every purpose I can think of, it's always better when you want to use a smaller font to place the cursor at the end of the last letter (no space), then change to the smaller font, type your space(s), then the letters you need to use. This way, you can make small changes to the spacing if you want to. If you have used a word processor in which codes could be embedded into text, then the principle will not be completely new to you. Version 3.0 of Fleet Street Editor allows FONT commands to be embedded in text.

You will get the flavour of all this if you try to reproduce the illustration of Figure 3.2. The first line of eyes has used Cairo, pressing the figure 2 to get this symbol (see your manual for the list of Cairo symbols). Pressing the RETURN key then gets the second line which start with one eye, then the font is switched to 10 point to type the spaces, to London to type the heading, and then back to 10 point for spaces. The other lines are dealt with in the same way. The problem then is to line up the right hand eyes, and then centre the words. This is done by deleting or adding spaces, and you can get a lot of help in this by putting the ruler on-screen. Select Page, then Use Rulers to do this, and you will see a ruler display with its own cursor showing the position of your text cursor. In the example, I lined up the right-hand eyes so that the centre of each eye was on the 5.75 mark on the ruler. Note, by the way, that both vertical and horizontal rulers appear, and each is scaled in inches and quarter-inches. Unless you are using a PC-compatible with a Hercules card, the vertical and horizontal scales will look different on screen but will correspond to equal distances on paper.

When the horizontal lining up is complete, you can then alter the spacing between lines either by moving the baselines or altering the leading. We have described how to alter leading previously, so in this example we can look at the movement of baselines. Select Baselines, then Adjust single. Click on the second line to produce the handles, and place the mouse pointer on the middle handle. Push the mouse button down (a half-click) and move the mouse to and fro so as to shift the line up or down as you require. Don't worry if the text disappears during this exercise. A certain amount of cut and try is needed until you get the spacing looking right but unless you have a train to catch you can spend as long as you like on this. When it all looks as you want it, then print away and see the results of your labours in their correct proportions.

Multiple columns

Though a lot of the type of work that shoestring desktop publishing is concerned with can use single wide columns, there are considerable advantages to be gained from the use of multiple columns. The main attraction is that the use of several narrow columns is visually more pleasing when graphics pictures are mixed with text, and this is a subject that we shall be developing in the following chapters. Even when your work uses no graphics, however, a wide sheet format can benefit considerably from division into columns, mainly because it allows for more interesting arrangement, particularly when you have a lot of comparatively small items. The appearance of a page consisting of a several sub-headings and one- or two-line text can be very displeasing and such a page is also quite difficult to read, as your eye tends to skip from one heading to the next.

Figure 3.3 shows an example of two-column work – remember that the illustration is restricted in width so as to fit the page size of this book as distinct from the nominal 8″ × 10″ text space that Fleet Street Editor allows with the Epson printer. This has started with defining the normal page as one of two columns, typing 2 in place of 1 in the Columns box of the Define Page menu. When making a page for yourself, you would, of course, define the

Our Local Lads Succeed Again!

First news this week is that our new member, Colin Fillpen, has already distinguished himself in his chosen career of rodent extermination technician. He has been successful in tracking down Methuselah, the rat which has caused panic in the Portwich housing estate for nearly a year now. Colin tells us that he used a Berriman Mark 17 improved trap, with a bait of rotting meat, having tried a variety of traps and baits before with no success. There is no doubt that everone concerned will be pleased at this excellent piece of work.

Another member, Jim Flauntit, has also covered himself with glory this week by making an appearance in the pages of the Mummerzet Bugle. Jim had been using his metal detector, built from a kit (the Hacklesberry Orion ZT7) on the banks of the Riddle, and his sharp ears had detected a slight signal. Digging revealed a signet-ring which is under investigation by our own Chas. Digitout, local historian and archivist. Chas. thinks that the ring could quite certainly be Victorian, but more investigation is needed.

Fig. 3.3 Two-column work, a style that is particularly suited to newspapers and some newsletters. The trick here is getting the headline.

margins that you wanted as well. The gutter size, fixed at 0.5" by default, can be left unless you feel that it needs to be changed. Since multiple columns really demand full justification, a J has been entered into the justification box.

With this preliminary work done, the screen is now a two-column screen. This means that when you type text, the text will jump to the next line as soon as it reaches the end of the left hand column, and you will add text in this column all the way to the bottom of the page before resuming again at the top, this time in the right hand column. This has implications when you are using the arrowed keys to move through the text, or when you are deleting. If you are near the end of the first column, for example, moving to the right with the right-arrow key will move you to the start of the next column, and it takes the screen a little time to find this position. The same applies if your cursor is on the top line of the right hand column and you are using the left-arrow key. Deleting text can also cause this same type of abrupt shift, with time being needed to rearrange the text on the screen. You should use the shift and delete keys slowly and carefully when you are at the start or the end of a column.

The selection of full justification also alters the way that words are placed on each line as you type. The first word of a line arranges itself on the left, the next on the right, and subsequent words appear at the right, forcing all but the first word to move left as you press keys. You can see by looking at the spacings when you are likely to need to put in a hyphen and a space to make a word split across lines. Practise with the example, typing the main text only and ignoring the headline.

When a piece of text like this has been typed, you will often find that one column is longer then the other. A little use of the Del key can move text from one column to the other until the columns are evened up. If one column has to be a line shorter than the other, always make the short column the one on the right, never on the left, unless you are deliberately making space for a picture or another sub-heading. In this example, you should *not* try to even up the columns yet, because this could cause problems with the placing of the heading. Adjustment of column lengths is best done using Baselines, a topic we shall look at later.

Adding the heading to this two-column layout is one of these actions that can have you dashing for the aspirins until you get used to the technique. It sounds simple enough in principle – you move both columns down, and then create a top line with a single column, then type in the heading. This is the equivalent of saying that to make a car all you have to do is to bend some steel around. Adding a headline *after* typing the columns is not so very easy, and it's much better to make provision for the heading in advance, by starting your text with two blank lines (two because you want to leave room for a heading in a larger size, not the 10 point of the main text. By doing this the difficult way, we can appreciate what is involved.

To start with, we definitely need a space for the heading, since the text starts in the first available line. Now we can make such a space by placing the cursor on to the start of the text and pressing RETURN twice to make two blank lines. When we do this, what will happen to the text? If the two columns of text already fill this page, then text will be shifted into a second page (it will, in fact, be held waiting for you to move to a second page). That creates further complications, so we'll assume for the moment that the text did not fill a page, and that making two blank spaces simply shifted two lines from the left hand column into the right hand column. You can then move the cursor to the start of the right hand column (using the mouse makes this easier, or you can use the F10 key and the arrow keys) and press RETURN twice, so making two blank lines in the second column. Once again, if your columns are long this may have caused an overflow, but for a short piece there will be no danger of this.

Now comes the crunch. When you select Baselines, you can see the column layout illustrated as a set of thick black lines, with the print represented as grey blobs. If we then click the mouse (or the F10 key) on one of the blank lines, we can then extend this line over the whole width of two columns. The question is, do we click on a line in the second column and stretch it to the left, or do we click on a line in the left hand column and stretch it right? The end result looks the same, but there is a very significant difference. If we click on the top line of the left-hand column and stretch it right (place the mouse pointer on the right hand handle and move the mouse to the right until the line end is in the same place as the line end for the second column) then this new line is regarded as a line in the left hand column, the first line of that column. To put a cursor in this line, you have to move to the top of the left hand column. If, on the other hand, you start with the top line of the right hand column and stretch this to the left, the line you get is treated as the first line in the second column. This means that if you adjust column lines, any heading on this line is likely to vanish to the bottom of the left-hand column, or that text from the bottom of the left hand column will come into this line. This can cause considerable difficulty with spacings between columns even if you do not alter line positions.

The rule, then, is to start at the left and stretch across right. You have now created a long first line, and you can put your cursor into it, select the font, size and style (usually bold for a heading) that you want, and type your heading. A single-word header will centre itself if you have selected full justification in your Define Page menu, but if you are using headlines of several words then you will have to use the Baselines, Adjust single, and Center menu choices. Next time you want to work with columns, start with two RETURN key presses so that you have a space at the start of the left hand column. If you have text spilling on to a second page, you can go on to edit it by using the Page menu to select the next page number to work on, then transfer the overspill text to the Clipboard and paste it into the next page. The main snag so far is that when we stretch a line across two columns in this way, there is still a normal line of the second column in place, and if text spills on to this line, it will appear superimposed on the heading. This can be dealt with by zeroing out baselines, a topic that we shall look at shortly.

A good test of your ability to work with columns and different sizes is illustrated in Figure 3.4. This is another address heading, but with the unusual feature of a large J that belongs to both parts of the name Julie James. The

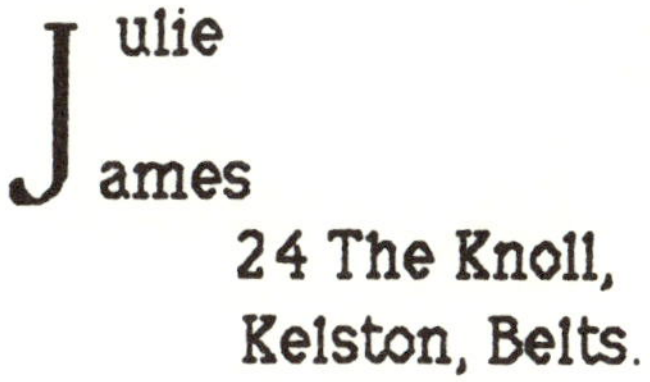

J ulie
 ames
24 The Knoll,
Kelston, Belts.

Fig. 3.4 A fancy letterhead, using columns to achieve the effect.

clue to the production of this logo is that two columns were selected. The large J is in one column, and the smaller print of the remainder of the names belongs in the second column. The smallest available gutter size of 0.2″ was used, and the baselines of the second column moved closer after the typing had been done. The baselines of the second column have also been moved vertically so as to line up with the top and the bottom of the large J. When you try this, think carefully when you want to make the size change, and on which line in the left hand column you will place the J. Make a note of what you have done, because this experience will stand you in good stead when you are faced with more difficult typesetting work with Fleet Street Editor.

Underlining and boxing

The use of bold and italic styles of type constitutes the only form of emphasis that is built into any font. This is different from most word processors, which allow you to select underlined text. Traditionally, when using metal type, underlining was carried out by placing lead alloy strips under lines, using strips that were wider than the leading strips, so that the line was inked and therefore printed. Fleet Street Editor creates underlining in the same way, and this introduces the first application of the symbols at the right hand side of the screen, the 'side tools'.

In Fleet Street Editor, underlining is a graphics action which is carried out with methods that are unfamiliar to anyone who has used only text editing. You can underline with a choice of four line thicknesses, and you can, of course, merge such lines together to make even thicker lines. Like the other graphics actions, underlining is easier to carry out using the mouse, though you can still use the F10/arrow key techniques that will be familiar to you by now if you are mouseless.

The example in Figure 3.5 shows a headline with and without underlining. To underline the second header:

(1) Place the mouse pointer over the line tool at the right hand side of the screen and click. The line tool is marked with a *diagonal* straight line.

A Heading

A Heading Underlined

Fig. 3.5 Illustrating the use of underlining for emphasis. Underlining requires one of the graphics 'side-tools', the line tool.

(Users with no mouse should substitute F9 and arrow keys).
(2) Place the pointer over the thickness of line you want to use and click again. The line thickness samples are in the lowest four boxes in the set of mouse tools. (Users with no mouse should simply substitute arrow keys.)
(3) The pointer on screen has now changed to a pair of cross-wires. Place the cross-wires where you want your underlining to start, at the left hand side under the headline.
(4) It's easier now to dispense with the mouse. Press and release the F10 key and use the right-arrow key to move the cross-wires until they are under the right hand side of the headline, then press F10 again. The cross-wires will leave a line behind them. You can use the mouse to do this, but it's much more difficult to keep the mouse moving in a straight horizontal line, though as long as the end of the cross-wires is in the same horizontal line as the start, the underlining will be horizontal, because a line drawn in this way is always straight. I just find it easier and quicker with the F10/arrow keys, since this makes it unnecessary to judge when a line is truly horizontal or vertical.

Using a box underline
| and you can put words into it too! |

Fig. 3.6 A box underline, showing also that words can be placed inside a box.

With the choice that you have for line thickness, you can underline any size of text that you happen to be using, and for additional emphasis you can use more than one line, separated or together. Another method of underlining is to use a box, illustrated in Figure 3.6. Drawing a box requires the use of the box tool, the box shape under the diagonal line. To underline with a box:

(1) Place the mouse pointer on the box tool symbol and click. (You can also select line thickness as for line drawing.)
(2) Place the cross-wires on the point which will be the top left hand corner of the box (under the left hand side of the headline).
(3) Press on the mouse button (half-click) and move the mouse to the point that will form the bottom right hand corner of the box. The box will appear on screen as you move the mouse.
(4) Release the mouse button when the box is of the size you want to use.

You can place small printing into the box if you want. This requires you to change size following the headline and type the message on a new line, then use Baselines to place the line of small print into the correct position of the box. Once again, you have to take some care over this action, because it's remarkably easy to find yourself printing in headline size when you think you are in 10 point. Emphasis with boxes can be effective, but like all such effects, it's useful only if it's not overdone.

Underlining and boxing forms an introduction to graphics, but one that we shall pursue no further here, because there are still a number of topics to look at that concern text alone. The next of these is the use of columns that do not extend for a full page, technically known as 'bastard' columns. When you select to use columns, you will normally find that you can type text into one column for the full extent of the page, after which the next column starts to fill up, and so on. For many purposes, this is not what you want – quite apart from anything else it could lead to some columns being far too long for easy reading, and you could end up with pages that required you to read from top to bottom several times if you wanted to read each story.

If you want to shorten column lengths, Fleet Street Editor provides for this by working with baselines. You know already how to lengthen or shorten a baseline. If you shorten a baseline and all the baselines below it until they disappear, a process called zeroing the baselines, then no text can be put on these lines and the text will have to jump to the next column. It sounds simple enough, but, as so often happens, takes more than a little practice to get right. If you simply zero out baselines to make two columns balance at the end of a page, then it's not too difficult. What takes a lot of time and patience, if you have not planned it well in advance, is producing pages such as Figure 3.7 in which stories have been set into these interrupted columns. This type of thing takes time, patience, and some experience of Fleet Street Editor.

We'll start with the simpler aspects of zeroing baselines. Start a page of two columns. Aim at producing a short report, like the three-liner (three lines on each of two columns) in the example. Set up your page dimensions with Define Page, making sure that you have specified two columns. When you are presented with the blank page don't start typing right away, but make the first line on the page a long line:

(1) Select Baselines, Adjust single.
(2) Click on the first line, right hand column.
(3) Put the pointer on the left side handle. Slide over to the right side handle. Release the mouse button. There should be an 'H' shape showing now in place of the baseline.
(4) This has zeroed out the first line of the second column so as to avoid text being put over the headline.
(5) Now select the first line of the left hand column. Click on the right side handle, and pull this over to the right so that it lines up with the right hand side of the second column.
(6) You can now select a font/size (example uses New York 18-point bold) and type your headline.

Spaniel missing, large reward

Jack, a five-year old Clumber Spaniel, is missing from his home in Wellington drive, near the sportsfield. Can any reader help?

More problems for team

Our tiddlywinks team has run into yet more trouble. After all the problems of last week, when they were evicted from the Brownie Hall, they have now been barred from the Green Dragon for 'riotous' behaviour. A new venue is now urgently sought.

The team, as you will recall from our action special issue last week, has covered itself in glory recently, and skipper Tom Bowla was said to be 'over the moon' at their prospects. He now feels 'sick as a parrot' at the treatment his lads have suffered.

Fig. 3.7 Using bastard columns, meaning columns which are each shorter than the page length.

(7) Press RETURN, and select a suitable font/size for your text – the example uses New York 10 point normal.

This has illustrated another use of a zero-length column. If you stretch the first line of your text along so as to cover the space of two columns, you will still have the first line of the second column present, though concealed. When you come to type on that line, the text will go on top of your headline. So far, the remedy has been to juggle with the baselines, shifting the first line up slightly so that it cleared the others, and then shifting the columns down (you have to take two shots at it because you cannot shift a baseline past another baseline nor beyond the page limits). This is clumsy, and it is much easier to zero out the unwanted line. A line that has been zeroed out is not an obstacle, text will simply ignore that line and proceed to the next.

The next problem is to place the text into the correct columns. This is considerable easier than you might think – the first time at least.

(1) Type your text normally, ignoring columns. The text will go into the left hand column under the headline. Don't worry about the spacing between the heading and the text, you can adjust this later.
(2) When your text is completed, count the lines and select a half-way line which you want to be the first line in the next column.

(3) Select baselines, Adjust below.
(4) Zero out the line which you have chosen as the first line in the next column. With the handles showing, click on the right hand handle and pull it across to cover the left hand one.
(5) This will zero out all the columns below it, because of your selection of Adjust below. The zeroed out columns below this are indicated by dots, and the column you have started with displays the 'H' sign.
(6) Return by clicking on Adjust below again. You should see the selected half of the text moved into the second column.

This type of action is so easy with Fleet Street Editor that you might wonder what the fuss is about. To find out, just try to reproduce the example of Figure 3.7. This starts with trying to restore some baselines so that you can type on to them. The advice on un-zeroing a baseline in the manual makes it look very simple, just select baselines, any suitable Adjust, point to the dot, click, and then pull the line out. What is not said, however, is that the line has to be pulled *left*, the mouse button released, and then the line restored in shape and size. Your natural action is to try to pull a line to the right when you are working on a left-hand column. This will cause a lot of frustration. You must pull left until the line is long enough to show three handles, and then adjust the right side, followed by the left side so that the baseline lines up again. Remember, if you have selected Adjust below, that all the lines under your selected line in the column will adjust in the same way.

Now whenever you restore baselines in the first column, your text from the second column will immediately pop back into the first column. This is entirely automatic, and there is nothing that you can do about it. If you then type your next lot of material, however (starting with a couple of blank lines to make way for the headline), then it will be inserted. If you find this insertion rather slow with V.2.0, you can speed up the action by using the Ins key to make the insertion, restoring the appearance of the text later. The piece of text from your second column, first headline, will remain at the end of the new text that you have typed in.

Now comes the cunning bit. Decide where the first column of the new text will end – the example shows this at the line ending 'now urgently sought'. Use the cut and paste command to put in the second column of the first set (starting with 'Wellington drive') following the last line of the new text in column 1. Now select Baselines, Adjust below, and zero out the line that starts 'The team, as you will recall'. This will have the effect of moving everything under it to column 2, with the portion on the lost dog in its correct place. The remainder of the tiddlywinks team copy may be too high up at present, but you can use Baselines Adjust below to move it down. You can then use Baselines Adjust single to extend the line for the heading, and put this in, using a suitable font and size. If, while using Baselines you find that text lines vanish

More Text Techniques   55

you can recall them with the Realign Text command.

It sounds complicated, and when you first try it, it can look complicated. The golden rule when you are trying to create this type of work is to have a plan laid out. With straightforward single-column work, which a lot of your

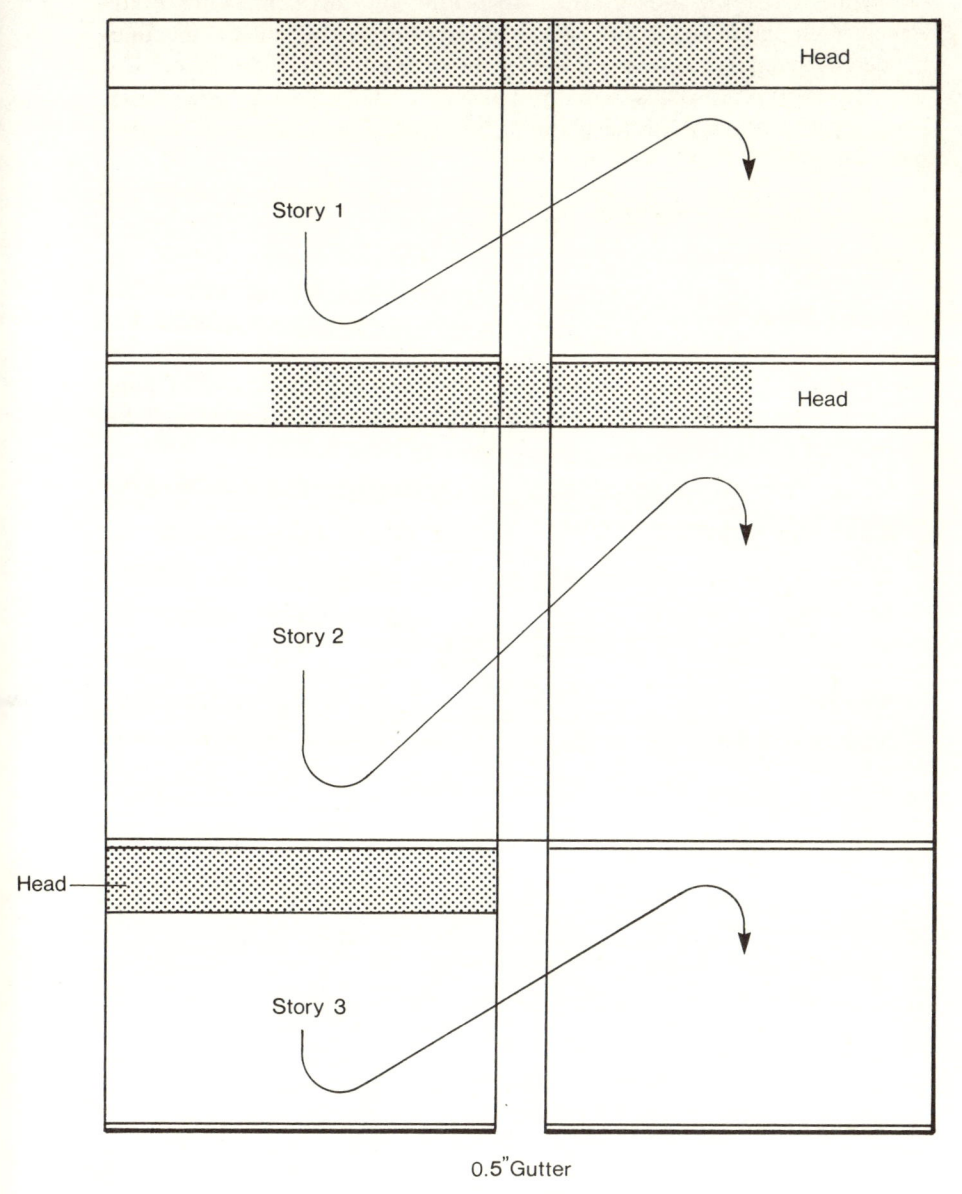

Fig. 3.8   A simple layout plan for columnar work.

output will be, you can get away with typing first and worrying about layout later. If you go in for multiple columns, particularly if you are trying to juggle with more than two columns, then planning becomes more important. You *can* work on a cut and try basis, but a lot of time will be saved if you plan out how your stories will look on the page before you start composing on the screen. Your planning does not have to be elaborate, it's the shape rather than the details that count here, as Figure 3.8 shows. Planning like this allows you to see where a column ends so that you know where to zero out the baselines, and later we shall see that such planning becomes essential when you want to place graphics in among your columns.

Shaped columns

There is nothing to stop you having two parallel straight-sided columns, but working with baselines can allow other interesting and useful effects to be achieved. Figure 3.9 shows one of these. A piece of text that uses two columns has been broken up with a box, in which material such as text can be inserted.

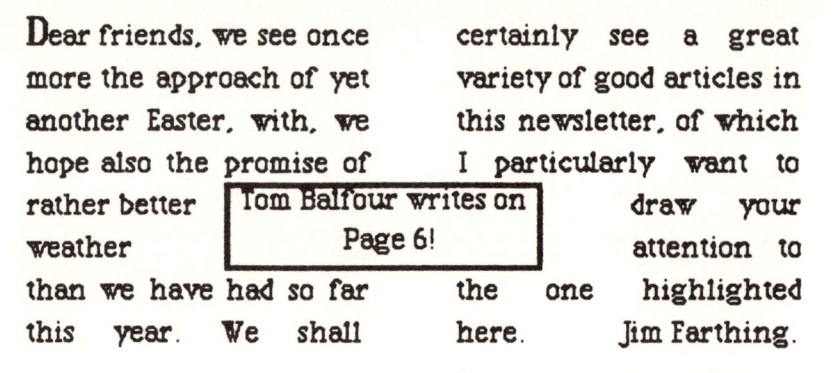

Dear friends, we see once more the approach of yet another Easter, with, we hope also the promise of rather better weather than we have had so far this year. We shall certainly see a great variety of good articles in this newsletter, of which I particularly want to draw your attention to the one highlighted here. Jim Farthing.

| Tom Balfour writes on Page 6! |

Fig. 3.9 Inserting a box between columns. The text in the box has been put in by graphics methods, because there are no baselines in this position.

The insertion of text in this example box is, to some extent, cheating, because we haven't dealt with how this is done, but the point I want to emphasise is the way that the columns have been shortened to make way for the box. This has been done as follows:

(1) Select Page, Define Page, and specify two columns along with the margins you want to use and full justification.
(2) Return to the screen for entry of text and before any text is entered, select Baselines, Adjust single.
(3) Working from the gutter position (between columns), shorten two lines

on the left hand column, then two lines on the right hand column. You do not have to repeat the command in order to do this, one selection of Adjust single allows you to move from line to line adjusting each.
(4) When the lines are adjusted (a good guide is to move one end handle to the centre handle), return to text entry, and type your text.
(5) Now make a guess at what line (below the short lines) you need to zero out to balance the text. This has to be a guess because it's difficult to predict the effect of the shorter lines in the second column.
(6) Using Adjust below, zero out lines. You can use Realign text to see how this looks. If the position is not correct, you can zero out a higher line, or restore your first zeroed line and try another lower one, depending on which way you need to move.
(7) Return to text. Now select the box drawing tool (one of the mouse tools at the side) and draw the box, pressing the mouse button down at the top left hand corner and releasing it at the bottom right hand corner.

This creates the box, with the columns making way for it. What you put into the box is a matter of graphics work, but you *cannot* just type in text because there is no baseline on which to type. The letters that you see in the box are, in fact, a form of *graphics* text, and this technique will be dealt with in detail in Chapters 4 and 5. It is obtained by selecting the second box down in the side set (the second A down the side-tools list), then using the mouse to put the cursor where you want it and typing. Text created like this cannot be manipulated by the ordinary methods of text typing, however, as you will find when you try it, and there is more on this topic in Chapter 4.

Figure 3.10 shows another application of working on lengths of baselines. In this example, the line and box tools have been used to make the crude shape of a house, more of the school of Picasso than of Gainsborough. Inside this framework, the Baseline Adjust single command has been used to create lines for text. At the start, a page of three columns was specified, so that by zeroing out unwanted columns and adjusting the length of others, a set of lines has been produced which occupies slots in the overall shape. If the text were better packed, it would be possible to erase the graphics outline and leave the text to show the shape alone. Here again, planning is needed so that you know in advance what you are going to put on each line. This example could have benefited from a smaller amount of leading between lines as well as from better drawing.

Tabulation and columns

Some material calls for tabulated work. You might, for example, be printing a page that shows sets of accounts, data for examination use, stock items, rota

For Your House

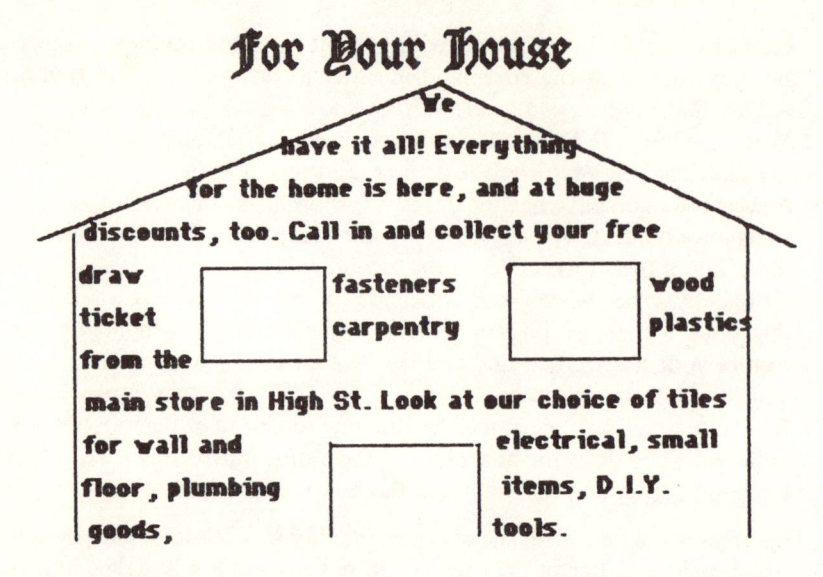

We have it all! Everything for the home is here, and at huge discounts, too. Call in and collect your free draw ticket from the main store in High St. Look at our choice of tiles for wall and floor, plumbing goods, fasteners, carpentry, electrical, small items, D.I.Y. tools, wood, plastics

Fig. 3.10 Shaping baselines so as to convey a message, in this case an advertisement for household DIY. This rough effort would need reworking before being used.

lists, anything that calls for several columns in which text, figures or a mixture of the two will be displayed. Now in this situation, it is important to choose the Courier font. Courier is a monospaced font, meaning that the characters, like those on a typewriter, are equally spaced. This is very important for working in columns, because in other fonts two names with the same number of letters might not take up the same space, and two numbers of the same size could also take up different amounts of space, making the tabular work look untidy. Remember that Fleet Street Editor does not allow you the use of the tabulation key on the PC machine, so that you have to keep your tables lined up by putting in spaces. In the example following, the page has been defined as having four columns, and these are zeroed out following the end of each section of data.

The example of Figure 3.11 shows the difference that the use of Courier, as compared to Geneva, makes to tabular work. The table of data about the planets of the solar system is shown in Figure 3.11(a) printed in Geneva. In this font, the decimal point look like short dashes (mainly because of the effect of a 'smoothed' printout with the dot-matrix printer) and they are not in line. The differences are, admittedly, small, but they make the table look slightly ragged, and the overall effect is poor. Contrast this with Figure 3.11(b), in which Courier has been used. The dots are still slightly elongated, but very precisely in line. Both printings have used bold and smoothed print, and the

(a)

Planet	Time of rotation	Orbit diameter	Eccentri- city
Mercury	000.241	00.387	0.206
Venus	000.615	00.723	0.007
Earth	001.000	01.000	0.017
Mars	001.881	01.524	0.093
Jupiter	011.862	05.203	0.048
Saturn	029.458	09.54	0.056
Uranus	084.01	19.2	0.047
Neptune	164.8	30.1	0.009
Pluto	248.4	39.4	0.249

(b)

Planet	Time of rotation	Orbit diameter	Eccentri- city
Mercury	000.241	00.387	0.206
Venus	000.615	00.723	0.007
Earth	001.000	01.000	0.017
Mars	001.881	01.524	0.093
Jupiter	011.862	05.203	0.048
Saturn	029.458	09.54	0.056
Uranus	084.01	19.2	0.047
Neptune	164.8	30.1	0.009
Pluto	248.4	39.4	0.249

Fig. 3.11 A set of tables printed using (a) Geneva, (b) Bold Courier.

appearance of the Courier is rather better using normal, and with standard print.

Fleet Street Editor allows you to use up to 4 columns. Though this is perfectly adequate for most types of work, it is not really well suited to tables for scientific use, in which 8 or more columns may be needed. For such work you have to abandon page columns, as defined in the Page menu, and simply create your own columns by spacing, as you would when using a typewriter. In the example of Figure 3.12, the page has been selected as consisting of a single column, and the figures (part of a set of compound interest tables) have been typed in Courier 12 point. The headings have been put in with graphics text, since it is very difficult to achieve a pleasing effect by manipulating baselines. Details of working with graphics text will be given in Chapter 4. The Courier font really comes into its own when you are working with text like this, and the only reason for considering any other font would be in order

n	$(1+i)^n$	v^n	s_n	a_n
1	1.1000	0.9091	1.000	0.909
2	1.2100	0.8264	2.100	1.736
3	1.3310	0.7513	3.310	2.487
4	1.4641	0.6830	4.641	3.170
5	1.6105	0.6209	6.105	3.791

Fig. 3.12 Using Courier in sets of more than 4 columns.

to use a point size that is not provided, since Fleet Street Editor Courier comes in only 10 and 12 point sizes.

Marginal notes

There are times when you need to put marginal notes into text, though this type of work seldom comes the way of the desktop publishing user. Just in case you need it, however, an explanation of the method by which the example of Figure 3.13 comes about might be useful to you. There are two ways in which these marginal notes can be inserted. One is to specify two columns, one of which is very narrow and used for notes. The alternative method is to specify one column with a wide margin and shift the left edge out into the margin where a note will be needed. We'll look at these in turn, starting with the two-column method, which is particularly suitable when you have a large number of marginal notes.

(1) Specify a page with two columns, and a narrow gutter, 0.3" or so.
(2) Zero out the left hand column.
(3) Expand the right hand column so that it is large enough to hold your text. Leave room at the left hand side for your notes, however.
(4) Type your text.
(5) Choose where you want the note. Expand out the line in the left hand column here. Some text will move into this line when you return to text entry.
(6) Type your note, usually in the smallest point size you have. Press the spacebar until any text that has moved from the main set has moved back again.

When you use this method, you can, of course, expand more than one line in the left hand column, so that your marginal note takes more than one line. You can also cater for having a different line spacing for marginal notes that take up more than one line. In general, this is better suited to applications

See page 55

> If you had to make a quick summary of what C had to offer, you could make it in this phrase: C is a language which combines the power of machine-code with the structure of a high-level language. In longer terms, C allows you the control over what the computer does that you normally associate with machine-code, and will generate compiled code that is almost as compact as machine-code from an assembler.
> (From *Simple C* by I. R. Sinclair)

Fig. 3.13 A marginal note inserted as shown in the text.

where you have a lot of marginal notes, several of which will need more than one line. The method needs some planning and a cool head, because you have the usual disconcerting problem of text moving from the first line or so of the main set into each margin line as you create it.

The second method is much simpler, but is better suited to applications in which a marginal note is seldom required.

(1) Define your page as consisting of one column only, using a wide left margin.
(2) Use Baselines Adjust below to move the left hand side of selected lines out to the margin sufficiently to make room for notes (allowing space for ten characters is a good working rule).
(3) Type your text, some of which will spill on to the space you have reserved for the marginal note.
(4) Move the cursor to the start of this marginal note line, select a suitable font/size and type the note. Use the spacebar to adjust the position of the main text.

In either example, you have to be sure that the cursor is in the correct place before you start typing, and you also need to be particularly careful if the marginal note is, as is normal, in a different point size. Once again, however, a little practice can make you quite proficient, and Fleet Street Editor is such that no matter what sort of mess you make at first, you can always get your text back to what you need.

Saving text

Normally when you save a page or a set of pages you do so as a .PUB file. This saves the work in its finished form, complete with layout, fonts, any graphics or special effects, just as you see it on screen and ready to print out. For some purposes, however, you do not want this. You might need to save the text only. This could then be used in a different format (different layout, fonts, graphics) on other pages, or possibly transferred to a word processor to be printed out in the ordinary way. There are two varieties of text-save action, requiring rather different approaches. Saving all of the text alone out of a single page (only a one-page save is allowed) is done from the Files menu, selecting the .TXT option from the dialogue box. You are not asked to specify a filename unless the page has not previously been saved, because if you are using a page that already exists as a .PUB file, the text is automatically saved as a .TXT file, using the same filename. Saving text in this way is useful mainly if the text is not too broken up on the page. Text which uses several columns will be returned in column form, which may not be the way that you want it. Any graphics text will *not* be saved in this way.

When you want such text back, you use the Text menu, selecting Get text. You will then see a list of the files with the extension .TXT so that you can select the one that you require. When you accept this text, it will be placed starting at the cursor position, so that you should be certain that the cursor is where you want it *before* you starting loading in the text. When the text is read in, it will take whatever font/size/style you are using currently, and you may have to edit the text to remove unwanted spaces. As noted above, loading text from two-column work back into a single-column page is going to cause you a lot of work with Cut and Paste to get the lines into the correct order.

The alternative method of saving text is for small pieces, like titles or other recurring text. If, for example, your newsletter contains in each issue some text to the effect that you have no connection with any commercial organisation, and if this disclaimer might be on a different page each time (where you can find space), then it makes sense to save such text as a .TXT file. Normally, headings and other material that goes into the same place in each edition would be saved as a .PUB file, saving the appearance of the page with only the recurring material typed in.

To save a small piece of text:

(1) Highlight the text, using the mouse or the F10/arrow keys.
(2) Select Text from the menu, then Save text.
(3) Supply a filename, which (for hard disk users) can include a path.
(4) Click on OK or press F1 to proceed.

Like the complete page, this section can then be read into another page, or it can be used by a word processor. All formatting information is lost, and this includes any graphics text. This is a point that needs to be emphasised, because when you look at a page, you cannot tell if a piece of text is plain text or graphics text. The distinction is important when you want to save small pieces of text, because graphics text cannot be saved as a .TXT file. This is because the creation of graphics text dispenses with the ASCII codes, leaving nothing that the machine can save.

Chapter Four
Starting With Graphics

The .MAC files

Using text by itself in your pages might be all that you want or need, but most users of desktop publishing will eventually see some advantages in adding some artwork to their pages. Artwork has the advantage of breaking up text and it can also be used to draw the reader's attention to a section. If your work requires a company logo to be used, then you have no choice but to deal in artwork, and though, like all effects, artwork can be overdone it can nevertheless be very effective when used in a restrained way. In this chapter, we shall look at the simple essentials of manipulating artwork with Fleet Street Editor, and later at how you can develop your own.

The artwork that is supplied along with Fleet Street Editor comes on a set of files with the extension of *.MAC*, an acknowledgement of the influence of the Apple Macintosh computer as the pioneer of desktop publishing with artwork. Each MAC file consists of a number of images packed tightly together, and the principle is that you extract the image that you want from the package. When you load an image into a page, you will normally load it as a file whose extension is *.ART*, not *.MAC*, so that this extraction process is a necessary one.

You can, however, load and print a complete MAC page. Your manual lists some of the MAC files, the files that exist on the Graphics Library disk of the 5¼" disk set or the 3.5" disk labelled Sampler and Graphics Library disk. Another set of MAC files is on the Sampler set, and these are LEISURE.MAC, BUSINESS.MAC, PERSONAL.MAC, PUBLICAT.MAC and HOLIDAYS.MAC. If you are using a hard disk, you can copy these over to join the other MAC files, but if you are using floppy drives, they are best left where they are. Since these extra files are not illustrated in the V.2.0 manual, you need to make your own illustrations:

(1) Start Fleet Street Editor with a blank page – do not even use Define Page unless you need to use odd-sized paper.
(2) Make sure that the appropriate disk is in the A: drive, or note which path is to be used (for the hard disk owner).

Starting With Graphics 65

(3) Select File, then Get Graphics.
(4) Select whatever MAC file you need. You will usually see a list of assorted files, but if you alter the Path box to A:*.MAC (floppy disk) or \FSE\PIX*.MAC (hard disk, assuming the use of a directory called PIX) then you will see only the MAC files.
(5) Load in the file by clicking on the Get spot.

This will allow you to see the whole of a graphics set. You can also print this out, because Fleet Street Editor automatically holds this graphics set as a *PUB* file. Since you only need to know what is contained in the set, you can use draft printing to get a quick impression, allowing one page for each MAC file.

For the moment, we shall make use of the set of MAC files that is on the Graphics disk in the $5\frac{1}{4}''$ and 3.5" disk sets. A few of these are 'anglicised' versions of graphics in the other sets (like the torn ticket labelled THEATRE instead of THEATER), but most of them are not duplicated. The first skill to acquire is the extraction of a single drawing from the set. As an example, we'll take the butler artwork from the Cartoons set, and show how to make this into a 'flyer' for an offer on wines.

We start by extracting the artwork:

(1) With Fleet Street Editor running, select the File menu, and specify Get Graphics. You will see the list of MAC files (assuming the correct disk is in the floppy drive or the correct path specified).
(2) Select CARTOONS.MAC in the usual way. Wait until the page is displayed on the screen.
(3) Move the mouse pointer to the art outline box. This is in the side tools strip at the right hand side, and is the box under the hand symbol, marked as a square with dotted sides. Click on this box (remember the usual F10/ arrow keys alternative).
(4) Place the mouse pointer at the top left hand corner of the artwork, in this case, the drawing of the butler. Press the mouse button down.
(5) Holding the mouse button down, move the mouse so that the pointer is at the bottom right hand side of the image. This is called 'mouse dragging' and its result will be to place a box around the image of the butler. Make sure that you have totally enclosed the image – you can start again if you need to.
(6) When the image is enclosed (it does not matter if part of another image also appears, but there is no problem in this example), click on the Art menu, and select Save Art.
(7) You will be asked for a file name, which in this case can be BUTLER. Clicking on OK will then save this artwork as a file called BUTLER.ART.

This completes the steps that are needed in order to separate out the image of the butler from the other artwork in CARTOONS.MAC. Having this image as an ART file now permits it to be read into a page. If you have words in a page, and you read in a complete MAC file you will delete all the words of the page, so that the selection has to be done over a blank page, before any text is written.

The art-outline dotted box is a very important part of all graphics work. The outline box is a graphics equivalent to highlighting of text – it marks the piece of artwork that you are working on. It is only when the outline box exists that you can move artwork around the screen, change its shape and size and perform other actions on it. When you make such an outline around an item in a MAC file, the outline (definition box) is saved with the item, and will appear again when you load in your ART file. Only one definition box at a time can exist, and when you create a new definition box you automatically delete any other one.

The next step is to create something that will use this artwork, and the logical answer is a wine-list. Figure 4.1 shows an example. The main title is in New York 18 point bold, right justified, and the list itself is in New York 12 point, also right aligned. The right alignment has been carried out using the Baselines Adjust below menu. When this part has been completed, the artwork can be added.

(1) Select Art, and then Get Art.
(2) From the list, select BUTLER.ART (this may be the only item on the list).
(3) When you return to your page, the text has greyed over, and a hand pointer is on the screen. This pointer indicates the position of the top left hand corner of the picture.
(4) Use the mouse (or arrow keys) to place the hand so that the picture will

This month's Wines....

Macon Blanc 1986	£4.85
Pouilly Fuisse '86	£8.75
Niersteiner '85	£6.22
Piesporter '86	£3.25
Mouton Cadet '85	£4.66
Chateau LaTour '85	£9.65

Fig. 4.1 A wine list fragment, making use of a piece of artwork.

Starting With Graphics **67**

be approximately where you want it. Click to place the artwork on screen.
(5) If the dotted frame (outline box) is still around the artwork, then you can place the hand at the edge and move the artwork by pressing the mouse button and moving the mouse. If the dotted outline has gone, you can make another one by pointing on to the dotted square tool and clicking, then drawing a new box around the butler. You can then go back and click on the hand symbol so as to be able to place the picture where you want it.
(6) To revert to normal text, place the mouse arrow in the top A box and click.

This description makes it all sound, in some respects, more difficult than it is, and it is really delightfully simple – something that is an underlying theme of Fleet Street Editor. The difficult part is ensuring that you stay within your page boundaries, because artwork does not necessarily respect any margins you have specified for text. Artwork obeys its own rules, and just what these rules are we shall find out in this and the following chapters.

Image sizes

The images that we can pick from the pages of MAC files allow us to select one for almost every application – but when we select an image its size is fixed. This is not inevitable, and Fleet Street Editor contains commands for scaling images. These need a little practice, because it is possible to distort an image considerably in this way. You might want this for comic effect, of course, but for other purposes, scaling an image needs to be done so that the same relative proportions are preserved. This makes the provision of Ruler lines particularly useful.

Consider, for example, the images in Figure 4.2, which have been taken from the ABODES.MAC set. The bungalow in (a) is the straightforward image, the other two have been obtained by copying the image and then rescaling it. You start this work by making a duplicate copy:

(1) Make sure that the image is still surrounded by its dotted definition box – if not, use the dotted-square tool, then return to the hand pointer.
(2) Click on Art, then on Duplicate. The hand symbol can then be placed wherever you want on the screen. To give yourself more space, press the PgDn key to take another section of the screen.
(3) Place the mouse pointer where you want the top left hand corner of the image to appear. Click to make the image appear.
(4) You can then use the hand pointer to pull the image, still in its dotted frame, the outline box, to wherever you want.

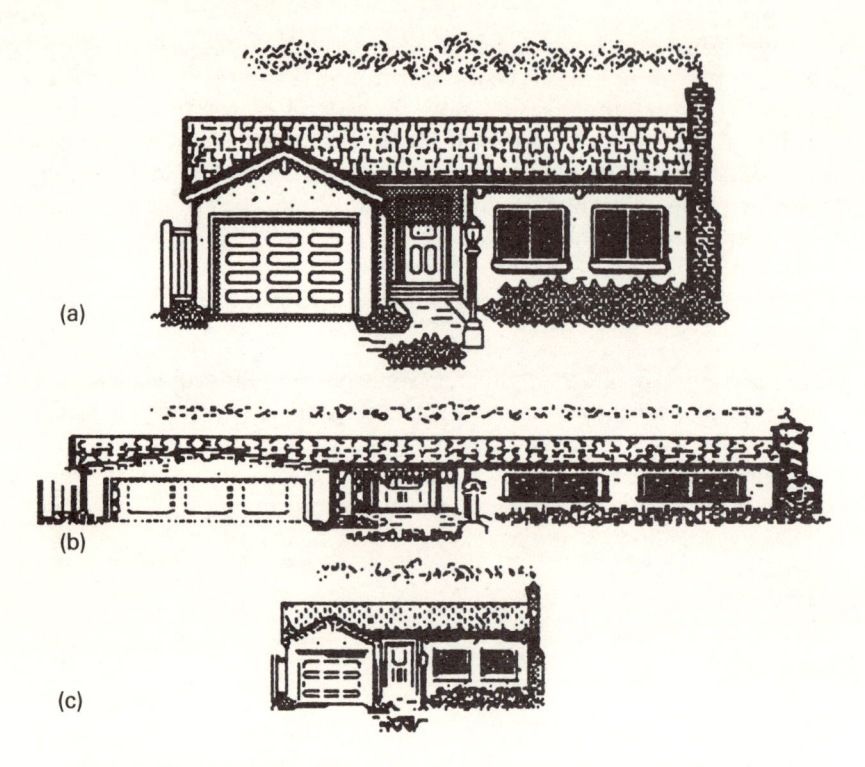

Fig. 4.2 Image resizing. (a) Original size, (b) widened, reduced height, (c) reduced in scale. The resized images are not perfect replicas of the original.

Now that you can make duplicates of artwork, try reading in the bungalow image from ABODES.MAC and make two copies. The next step is to make these copies resized, one in one direction, the other more evenly.

(1) Place the outline box around one of your duplicates. Remember that this is the mouse tool under the hand symbol.
(2) Click on Art, then on *Resize*. You will see 'handles' appear in each corner of the dotted box.
(3) By moving the mouse pointer to a handle, and pressing the mouse button (half-click) you can drag the corner sideways, up or down to alter the height or width of the image, so altering its size.
(4) Keeping the width the same and reducing the height creates a 'Cinemascope' image, as in Figure 4.2(b).
(5) Reducing both dimensions gives an image that retains the same proportions, Figure 4.2(c).

Resizing *does*, however, introduce other distortions, particularly when any dimension is reduced. As you can see in the examples, the Cinemascope image

Starting With Graphics 69

has been considerably distorted – look at the number of panels in the garage door and at the side gate. Even when the scale is better preserved, much detail is lost, as Figure 4.2(c) shows. Resizing is useful – but only when you have some experience and realise what the limitations can be. In Chapter 5 we'll look at the Magnify technique which allows you to correct some of the distortions caused by resizing.

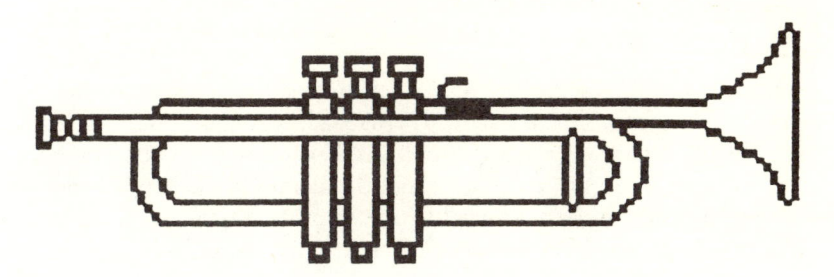

Fig. 4.3 An image resized, showing that the small steps that form the curves in the original become large and noticeable steps in the resized version.

Don't assume that resizing upwards will make more detail appear. As the example of Figure 4.3 shows, the result is to show that the curves are made from straight line steps. In general, the best size for an image is its original size, and though a limited amount of resizing can be useful, it is not a cure-all which allows you to put an image in anywhere. As it happens, resizing an image upwards can sometimes be combined with methods of 'retouching' the image, but that's something we'll come on to when we are looking at the Magnify command. The main use for the Resize command is to allow an image to fit into a space that has been allocated for it, and a few images in the MAC sets are available in two or more sizes to allow you to select whichever needs less resizing for the application that you have in mind.

The Flip commands

Fleet Street Editor contains two other commands, the flip commands, in the Art set that are useful for many types of images. As the name suggests, one of these allows the image to be flipped (turned around) horizontally, the other permits a vertical flip. Version 3.0 of Fleet Street Editor allows a set of 90 degree turns to be carried rather than just these two flip commands. The effects can be very useful if the artwork you want is, for example, facing the wrong way or if you want to have mirror images.

Fig. 4.4 A letterhead that uses a graphics image consisting of a resized image and its duplicate which has been flipped horizontally.

Figure 4.4 shows a design for headed notepaper, using penguins. The penguins are taken from the HOLIDAYS.MAC file, and the text is in London font. The important point here, however, is how to produce two symmetrical penguin images, because if you carry out the actions in the wrong order you will run into difficulties with symmetry. Another important point in this example is how to remove an unwanted part of an image.

(1) Use Files, Get Graphics to read in HOLIDAYS.MAC (on the Sampler disk of the $5\frac{1}{4}''$ set).
(2) Use the outline box to enclose the penguins image. In doing this you will probably enclose part of the adjacent reindeer or JOY images.
(3) Save the ART file in the usual way.
(4) Prepare your page, with the lettering in London font.
(5) Use Art, Get Art to read the PENGUIN.ART file.
(6) Place the penguin image at the left hand side of your page. Position it with the hand symbol.
(7) Use Resize to make this image a size that will fit the page.
(8) Remove unwanted pieces from other images. Select the eraser tool (side-tools, eighth down (just above the line thickness set)). Place the square pointer over any part to be erased, press the mouse pointer down and move the 'erasing square' over the parts to be deleted. Release the mouse button to move to another portion of the image.
(9) Now select duplicate, and make another image at the opposite side of the page.
(10) With the outline box on this duplicate, select Flip Horizontal to make the penguins face the other way.

The important part here is to do all the positioning and resizing *before* the duplicating and flip actions. If you have to resize two separate images you are unlikely to get them both of the same size – you might, of course, prefer it this way. Resizing, you will note, works well with images like this in which the outline is not too regular. The positioning of the images is aided by using the Page menu Use Rulers command, so that the cursor position can be compared with the scaling of rulers at the top and the side of the screen. The only problem with this is that the ruling is rather coarse. This can be improved by using, instead of Rulers, a grid pattern.

The grid pattern is obtained by selecting Page, and then Move in Steps. The dialogue box that appears asks you to specify the step size, with the standard figure of 0.25 appearing. This means that the grid which will appear will have 0.25" squares, and on the Amstrad screen (and on any machine that does not use the Hercules card) each square of the grid will look rectangular, with its height twice as large as its width. The importance of these squares is that they correspond to printed sizes, so that they can be used to line up images very precisely. The smallest size of step that you can use is 0.12", and the largest is 1.0" – it would be rather unusual to need the larger sizes. One of the advantages of using the grid of steps is that it exists on each screen page, allowing you to line up images in the same vertical line even when one of the images is out of sight, off the screen. Any action that involves movement will move in steps equal to the spacing of the grid lines, so that you might need to turn the effect off (click again on Move in Steps) before you moved the cursor or dragged images. If, however, you are trying to line up duplicated images, the use of Move in Steps can be very useful, as it allows faster and more precise movement.

Image position

The position of an image on a screen page is adjusted, as we have seen, by using the mouse or the arrowed keys to move the hand symbol after this symbol has been 'attached' to the definition frame around the image. The attachment is done by the action of pressing the mouse button (half-click) and keeping the button pressed while the movement is carried out. As non-mouse users will know by now, the corresponding action is to press the F10 key, move the hand, then press F10 again.

Things are slightly different when you want to copy or move an image to a different screen page. The ordinary method of movement within a page does not extend to other pages (in which respect graphics work is little different from text), and to copy or move an image to another page you have to make use of the Copy, Cut, Paste or Duplicate commands. These are *not* the commands from the text menu, however, but from the Art menu. The action is identical, however. To move an image to another page, page 2 in this example:

(1) Make sure that the image has the definition box around it to mark which image you want to work on.
(2) Select Art, then Cut. This will remove the image, storing the pattern in a spare piece of memory (the Clipboard).
(3) Move to the new page. Select the Page menu, and from this choose Jump to Page. Specify the page number (2 in this example), and click on OK.
(4) Click on Art, and select Paste. Select the Hand pointer tool.
(5) Use the Hand pointer to move to the place where you want the top left hand corner of the definition box to appear, and click the mouse button.

Other manipulations

While we are working with these images we can take some time over the other ways in which images can be manipulated, concentrating on the vertical flip and the inversion. Figure 4.5 shows an image inverted. This does not mean inverted in the sense of turned upside down (that's vertical flip), but in the sense of exchanging black for white and white for black, like a photographic negative. The effect can be a useful one if you are advertising photographic products, but for other purposes it is often more useful for graphics text than

Fig. 4.5 An image and its inverted version. Inversion should not be confused with vertical flip action.

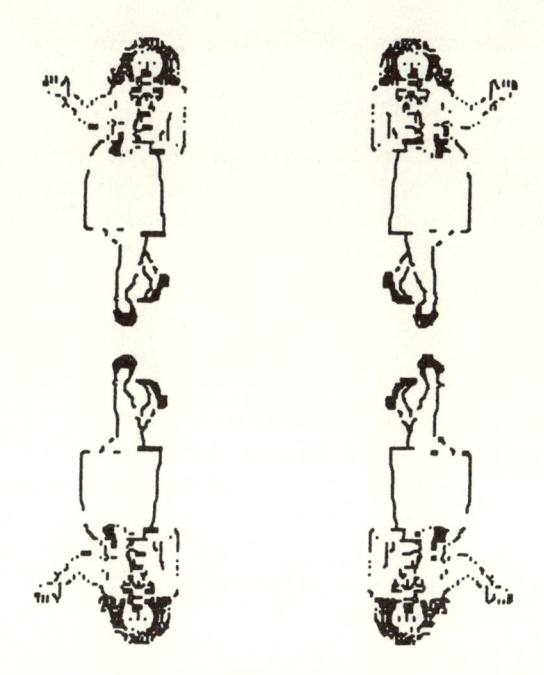

Fig. 4.6 A set of images produced by duplication along with vertical and horizontal flip actions.

for straightforward images. Some very interesting effects can be obtained when a negative image is operated on with the pencil and eraser tools, but that's for later.

Meantime, take a look at the effect of the flip horizontal and flip vertical commands, or their equivalent in V.3.0, the 90 degree turn commands. Figure 4.6 shows four images of the Peter-Paul Rubens Down-with-anorexia school of artwork. These have been produced by the use of Duplicate (Art menu) and the two Flip commands. The order of production was as follows:

(1) The image was extracted from the DISPLAYS.MAC file, and saved as GIRL.ART.
(2) This image was then read into a page, and reduced in height and width. The reduction was not proportional, resulting in a fuller figure, as they say. (This image can be improved (retouched) by using the Magnify command covered in chapter 5.)
(3) The image was duplicated to a position on the right. This image was then flipped horizontally.
(4) The flipped image was then duplicated to a position below, and then flipped vertically.

74 *Desktop Publishing on a Shoestring*

(5) The first image was surrounded with the definition box, and duplicated to a position below.
(6) This image was then flipped vertically.

The result of all this is a set of images that look like mirror (appropriate for Mirrorsoft) images. Version 3.0 of Fleet Street Editor also allows 90 degree turning, so that you can get horizontal images, hand up or hand down. This makes the turning command of V.3.0 considerably more versatile than the flip commands of V.2.0.

Merging images

You are not confined to using single images from the MAC pages, because the image handling methods that make use of the art definition box allow images to be merged as you please. While the dotted image definition box exists around an image, you can do as you please with that image, inverting, flipping, resizing and moving it as you choose. Even when you move that image over another you have complete individual control for as long as that definition box remains around your image. If, however, you bring two images together in this way and then remove the box (by clicking on the text A, for example, or by drawing another box somewhere else) then the images merge, and cannot be separated unless the nature of the images permits this. You can always, however, separate a graphics image from ordinary text, because the definition box, even if it encloses some text, has no effect on text.

Take as an example, Figure 4.7, The picture frame has been taken from

Fig. 4.7 Merging images. The frame has been taken from one MAC set, the chorus line from another. These images can be separated again.

Starting With Graphics **75**

DISPLAYS.MAC and the chorus line from COLUMNS-3.MAC. The merging has been done by placing the frame on screen first, and then the chorus line, which will still have its definition box around it. The chorus line image has then been moved inside the picture frame, using the hand pointer, then the box has been removed (click on the top A in the side tools) and the page printed.

Now this is an example of a merged pair of images that *can* be separated. Since the chorus line image fits inside the frame, not touching any part of the edge, you could draw a definition box around it again and move it out without affecting the picture frame. This cannot be so easily done in the example of Figure 4.8(a). In this case, the ship and the musical stave have been merged, perhaps to indicate a musical tour. Placing a definition box around the ship now will inevitably include part of the stave, and if the box is now moved, a hole will be left in the original shape as Figure 4.8(b) shows. When you amalgamate shapes like this, you have to be certain that the merged shape is as you want it before you remove the definition box. If you need to make a change after that, then you will have to start with the two (or more) ART images again.

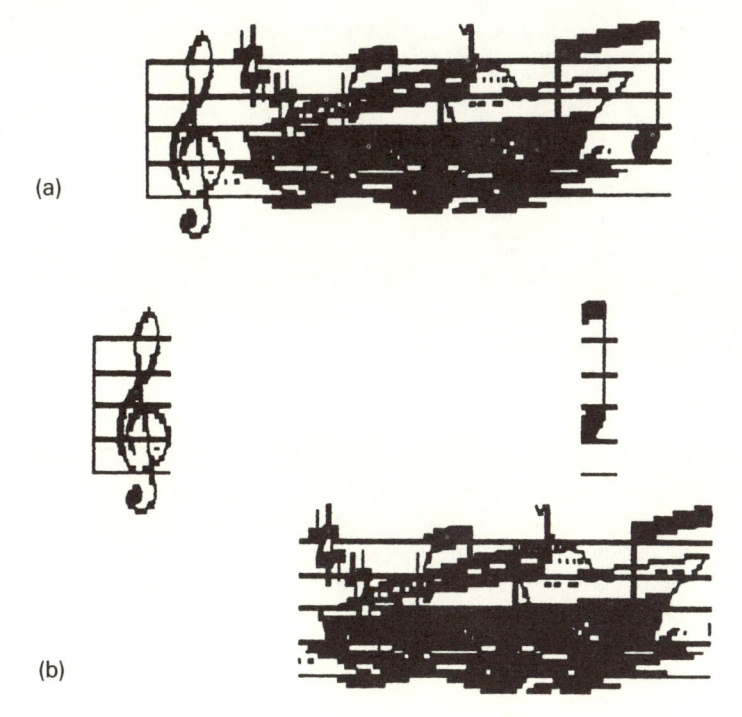

Fig. 4.8 (a) A ship image merged with a musical stave image. (b) What happens when you try to separate the images.

Fairly Fastidious Golf Club

The following are the new rules regarding dress in the clubhouse.
The following attire is strictly not allowed –

Men	Women
Shorts	Trousers
T-shirts	Blouses
Open-necked shirts	Headscarfs
Raucous ties	Short skirts
Sandals	High heels
Unsupported socks	Body stockings

– or any casual or 'sporting' attire of any nature.

Fig. 4.9 An image used as a heading, with text following it. The text has used normal methods, pressing RETURN to get a line under the graphics.

Words and images

It would be unusual to make any use of these graphics images on their own, and you will almost inevitably want to place words along with the images. The most straightforward and simple way of doing this is illustrated in Figure 4.9. The images have been placed here at the head of the paper, and when the text has been entered, it is placed further down the sheet, clear of the artwork. This is done as follows:

(1) Prepare the images in the usual way, using in this example two ART files taken from LEISURE.MAC and DINGBATS.MAC.
(2) Use the Start Over command to clear the page, and then use Define Page to settle the dimensions for your page.
(3) Put in the graphics from the ART files. The mug image is placed at the left hand side, and then Duplicate used to make a copy at the right hand side. This copy is then flipped horizontally. The golfer image is put in and duplicated twice more.
(4) Text entry is selected, placing the mouse cursor on the top A in the side-tools and clicking. This leaves the text cursor at the top left hand corner of the page, with no effect on the artwork.

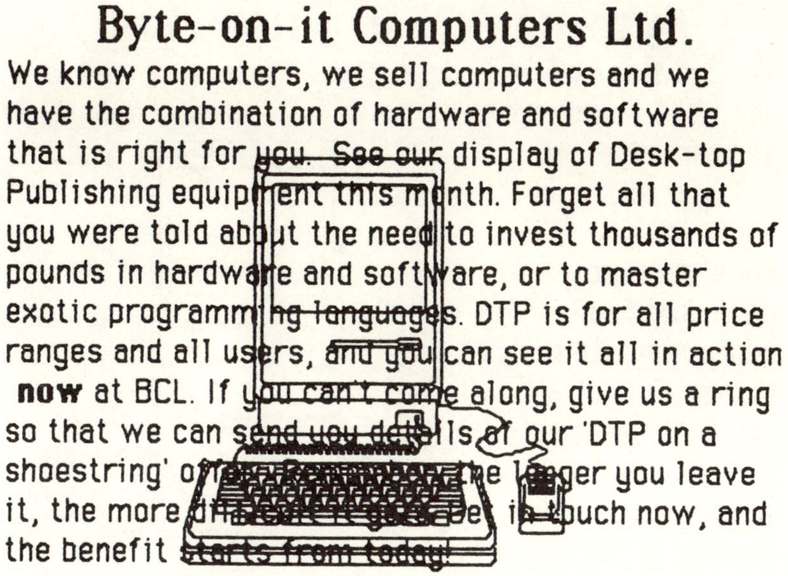

Byte-on-it Computers Ltd.

We know computers, we sell computers and we have the combination of hardware and software that is right for you. See our display of Desk-top Publishing equipment this month. Forget all that you were told about the need to invest thousands of pounds in hardware and software, or to master exotic programming languages. DTP is for all price ranges and all users, and you can see it all in action **now** at BCL. If you can't come along, give us a ring so that we can send you details of our 'DTP on a shoestring' offer. Remember, the longer you leave it, the more difficult it gets. Get in touch now, and the benefit starts from today!

Fig. 4.10 Text and graphics can be merged, with effects that can be striking, but difficult to read.

(5) The RETURN key is used to space the text cursor down until it is on a line clear of the artwork. An alternative is to zero out the first few lines that conflict with the artwork.

(6) Text can now be entered, using the normal range of fonts, styles and sizes.

A large number of requirements for desktop publishing need no more than this, but it often adds to the appeal of a printed page if the text and the graphics are more closely mixed. Figure 4.10 shows an example. The computer image has been taken from the file DESKITEM.MAC and put on to the screen after defining the page size. The text has then been typed, and, as you can see, the text goes on to the page ignoring the graphics altogether. This *can* be very eye-catching, but the problem is that a chunk of the text is unreadable where the keyboard of the computer makes the density of the graphics greater. Some types of line graphics can mix very well with text, however, and the use of text over graphics then looks quite eye-catching without obscuring the message.

There are various ways around this type of problem, and one is the use of PictureWrap. When the artwork is placed on the screen, it is placed either to the right or to the left of each column, and the text is automatically wrapped around it. To be more precise, the text is wrapped around the definition box rather than round the graphics shape, so that the hole in the text is always rectangular, though it does not necessarily look rectangular if the text is not

Byte-on-it Computers Ltd.

We know computers, we sell computers and we have the combination of hardware and software that is right for you. See our display of Desk-top Publishing equipment this month. Forget all that you were told about the need to invest thousands of pounds in hardware and software, or to master exotic programming languages. DTP is for all price ranges and all users, and you can see it all in action now at BCL. If you can't come along, give us a ring so that we can send you details of our 'DTP on a shoestring' offer. Remember, the longer you leave it, the more difficult it gets. Get in touch now, and the benefit starts from today!

Fig. 4.11 Using PictureWrap to make the text wrap around the definition box of the graphics image.

fully justified. What this does, in effect, is to make each baseline stop at the edge of the definition box for the artwork. This applies whether the definition box is visible or not. You can put in the picture and wrap the text as illustrated, or alternatively put in the text and then apply the picture, at which time the text will wrap if PictureWrap is selected.

Figure 4.11 shows this type of treatment, with the image placed to the right of the page. The procedure is:

(1) Define the page and place the image at the right hand side. Use Rulers (from the Page menu) to guide you on positioning.
(2) When the image is in position, use the Page menu to select PictureWrap.

Starting With Graphics 79

The tick against this choice indicates that it is switched on and will remain on until it is selected again.

(3) Now select text entry (the top A on the toolkit) and type the text. The text will automatically wrap around the (invisible) definition box of the artwork.

The only snag here is that PictureWrap works on a single image only; if you have more than one graphic on a page you have to take your text round the first, using PictureWrap, then put a definition box around the second image, select text entry, and then continue typing. You have to make sure also when you do this that the first image that you come to is the image that was left with a definition box, because it's the definition box that PictureWrap obeys.

The use of PictureWrap is confined to wrapping around one side of the artwork only. This can be the right hand side or the left hand side, but you

Byte-on-it Computers Ltd.

We know computers, we sell computers and we have the combination of hardware and software that is right for you. See our display of Desk-top Publishing equipment this month. Forget all that you were told about the need to invest thousands of pounds in hardware and software, or our 'DTP on a shoe-string' offer. Remember, the longer you leave it, the more difficult it gets. Get in touch now, and the benefit starts from today! to master exotic programming languages. DTP is for all price ranges and all users, and you can see it all in action now at BCL. If you can't come along, give us a ring so that we can send you details of

Fig. 4.12 Text can be wrapped around only one side of an image, unless two columns of text are used. This leads, however, to the sequence of text becoming very odd.

cannot take a single column and split it with PictureWrap so that the words split on each side of the picture. If you want the appearance of an image in the centre of your page with words on each side, then you have to use two columns when you define your page, as Figure 4.12 illustrates.

This example has been heavily worked on. The page was defined as having two columns, but the second column was zeroed out both above the image and below it. The lines of the first column were then extended above and below the image, so that these lines are full-length. The snag is that the text does not follow on logically – you have to jump from the last line to the top of the second column to the right of the image. This would have looked better with the image lower, so that there were no long lines under the image. You can put a definition box around the image, switch on PictureWrap, and pull the image down. The text will then make space for the image, establishing where it is best sited. You need to do this early on, however, before you do any kind of adjustments with Baselines. As long as PictureWrap is switched on, the text will not extend over the edges of the definition box.

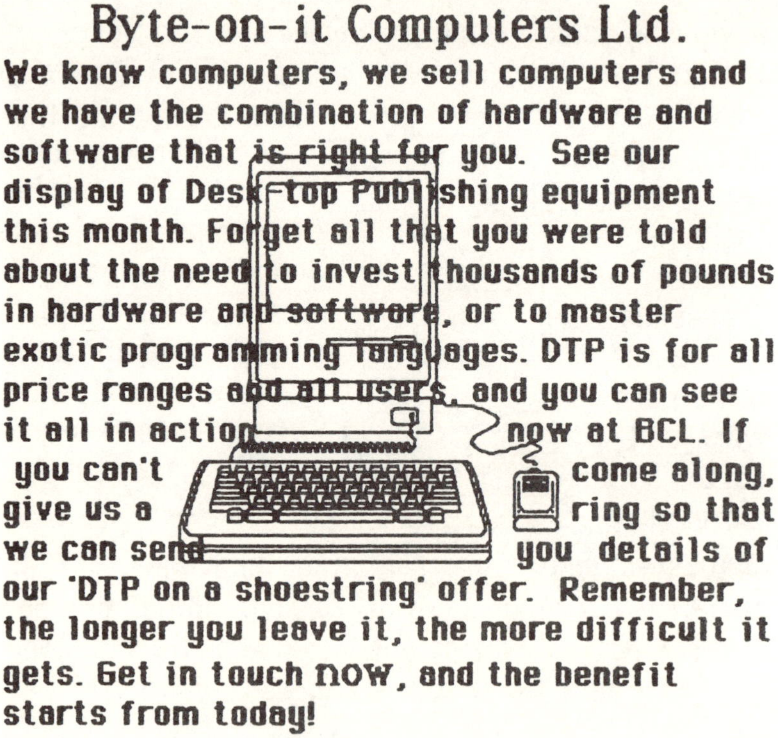

Byte-on-it Computers Ltd.

We know computers, we sell computers and we have the combination of hardware and software that is right for you. See our display of Desktop Publishing equipment this month. Forget all that you were told about the need to invest thousands of pounds in hardware and software, or to master exotic programming languages. DTP is for all price ranges and all users, and you can see it all in action now at BCL. If you can't come along, give us a ring so that we can send you details of our 'DTP on a shoestring' offer. Remember, the longer you leave it, the more difficult it gets. Get in touch now, and the benefit starts from today!

Fig. 4.13 A compromise method, with some text being typed over the image, and the rest spaced out so as to avoid the denser parts of the image.

You can force the text to go over these limits, by working on the baselines, though re-aligning the text will put things back as they were. In the illustration of Figure 4.12, the text in the left hand column has been adjusted in this way, showing the contrast with the unadjusted text on the right hand side. This can be tedious, but it can produce very good-looking results if the image has been suitably placed with respect to the text. By far the best way of running text around each side of images is to use graphics text, positioned by way of the mouse so that baselines are dispensed with altogether.

Sometimes, the simplest options can be the most effective. Figure 4.13 shows the same image and text again, but with a page defined as having one column of normal width. The text has been taken through the image where the image density is light, but at the keyboard, the text line is split. This has not been done by any fancy techniques, simply by the use of the spacebar. For example, the cursor was placed at the start of the word 'now' and the spacebar pressed until the word moved to the right of the mouse cable in the image. Other lines were treated similarly, and the whole text was put into bold face to show up better over the image. Note that the change to bold face *must* be made before changes are made to the spacing, because bold face is wider than normal text in this font (in most fonts except Courier), so that if you space out your words and then alter the face, you will find that your spacings are incorrect. Note, incidentally, that the word 'now' has been emphasised by being put into another font and size. This was previously emphasised by having this as the only word in bold face, but with all of the text now in bold, another method of emphasis is needed.

Graphics text

So far, our use of graphics has been of images taken from MAC files, put into ART files and then used in pages. Fleet Street Editor also allows you to use graphics text which, as the name suggests, is text that obeys the rules of graphics rather then the normal rules of text. Graphics text allows a lot of interesting effects to be achieved, and not only because of the type of graphics actions that we have been looking at here. Any text which is created as graphics text is totally free from Baselines, and can be overprinted by normal text. The liberation from Baselines also allows line spacings that are less constrained than is the case when we use normal text.

As an example, look at Figure 4.14. The page has been defined, and then Graphics text selected by clicking the mouse pointer on the second A in the toolbox set. Once graphics text has been selected in this way, you have the same choice of fonts, sizes and styles as you have with ordinary text, but you have much more freedom on how you arrange the text. To start with, you will see that the page boundaries that you set have been ignored – they belong with

> NOW LOOK HERE

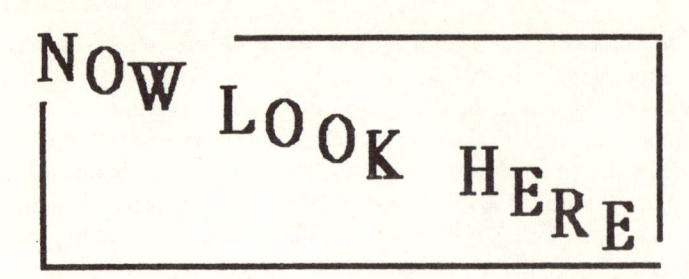

Fig. 4.14 Graphics text in use – each letter can be positioned by using the mouse to place the cursor before typing the letter.

text, not with graphics. If you want to keep within these boundaries you will have to move your graphics about to suit, using graphics methods. New York 24 point has been selected, and the first letter typed, then the cursor moved by moving the mouse cursor and clicking. The second letter is then typed, and so on. The text could be made more even by drawing a diagonal line first, but for this simple example it's easier to see what is being done if guidelines are omitted. After all the letters have been entered in this way, the straight lines are drawn using the straight line drawing method described earlier. To recap, you select the straight line box (labelled with the \ mark), place the mouse cursor at the point where the line starts, then press the mouse button and move the line to where you want it to end, then release the mouse button.

The effect of text like this can be very useful, and if you make particularly elaborate examples you should save them as ART files which might be useful later. Creating new artwork is always hard work, though there are many useful programs to assist in such work, and when you have spent some time on a piece of artwork you should always file it, retaining a printed copy to remind you of what it looks like. Several of the pieces of artwork in the MAC files are, in fact, little more than graphics letters, and you can probably think of examples that would be more useful to you. In this example, the positions of letters could be adjusted individually by placing a definition box around a letter and using the hand pointer to move the letter.

Figure 4.15 shows a combination of graphics image and graphics text, illustrating that graphics text can be run along a curved surface. As it happens, you don't have many curved surfaces in your MAC files because curves print out looking rather ragged, and look even worse on the screen. In this example, the artwork has been put on to the screen, and the graphics text selected. Geneva 10 point has been used for the text, positioning the cursor with the mouse before each letter is typed. This is not always easy, and can involve some hard work (like modifying the bulb from US screw-in type to UK plug-in type!). Once again, if you create really memorable images in this way, you should save then separately as ART files which can then be used in other pages.

Fig. 4.15 Image and graphics text combined – useful for some very striking effects.

Working with graphics text can be an art form in its own right. Figure 4.16 shows a play on the letter A. The large A was in this case obtained by using a 24 point New York and resizing. This was deliberately preferred to the use of a 36 point letter so that the stepped nature of the sloping sides would be emphasised. These steps create convenient niches into which the smaller letters fit, in New York 14 point. The border has been drawn first with a thin line and then with a thicker line.

Inversion effects

Inversion, the interchange of black and white, has a greater part to play in graphics text work than in images, because so many striking and yet legible effects can be accomplished in this way. The simplest application is to type a heading in graphics text and then invert it. This has its maximum impact if the black area is not too large, so you need to draw the definition box very closely around the heading before using the Inversion command.

Fig. 4.16 Using graphics text, along with resizing, to create a play on the letter A.

SAVE OUR SHORELINE

SAVE OUR SHORELINE

Fig. 4.17 A headline and its inverted counterpart. Inversion is often more useful for graphics text than for other artwork.

Figure 4.17 shows two headlines, both using New York 18 point normal, but with one inverted. The amount of solid black in the inverted version makes it much more eye-catching. This can be used to good effect when text is placed inside a graphics casing, as we'll look at later in the following chapter. Inversion should be used only for the larger sizes of type, because the white areas do not stand out so well against the black background in the smaller sizes. I feel also that lower case letters do not have the same impact as capitals when inverted, but this is very much a matter for your own judgement and taste.

Inversion can, of course, be combined with other effects, and Figure 4.18 shows it used with resizing in the vertical direction. This has the effect of considerably distorting the phrase, and you have to balance the eye-catching effect of this against the loss of legibility. When you use distorted letters like this, you should place the same message in different words underneath (or close by, at least) so as to ensure that no-one loses the message because they don't feel inclined to read the headline. In this example from some time ago, the message was obviously read and understood.

Distortions of letters are always a problem. I have seen posters in such

STOP THE RATES ROBBERY!

Rates are guesswork! Support alternatives NOW

Fig. 4.18 Inversion and resizing used to create distorted letters, useful to attract attention, but not always easily readable.

Reflections

Fig. 4.19 The appearance of reflection made using a duplicate which has been flipped and brought up to touch the original.

grotesque gothic print that the message was almost completely illegible, and even when the main message is in a better font, many people will not read on. There is such a thing as optical fatigue brought on by too many typographical tricks, and the use of desktop publishing has, if anything, increased the problem. The trouble is that typographical tricks are very simple to perform now, so that every user of desktop publishing is tempted to use a large number of artifices in each publication. This is not an encouragement for readers, and the mark of good desktop publishing should be restraint – unless you deliberately wish otherwise. As always, it's experience that counts.

With that homily delivered, let's look at some ways of making a heading eye-catching without reducing the readability of the main part. Figure 4.19 shows a heading for a firm called Reflections (a name that is very popular). The heading has been typed in New York 24 point, then duplicated. The duplicate has been inverted, then dragged over so that it lies exactly under the original. This is just one example of a heading which would be very difficult to produce in the days of metal type, but which is ridiculously easy with desktop publishing, and with Fleet Street Editor in particular.

A heading like this should be kept for names that suggest reflection, (like Mirrorsoft?), because the image becomes a pointless one if it is used for something that has no connection with reflections, like the Old Sarnians Rugby Club. When you make up fancy headings of this type, there has to be a reason for the form that you adopt.

Figure 4.20 shows how the effect of a reflection in water can be obtained.

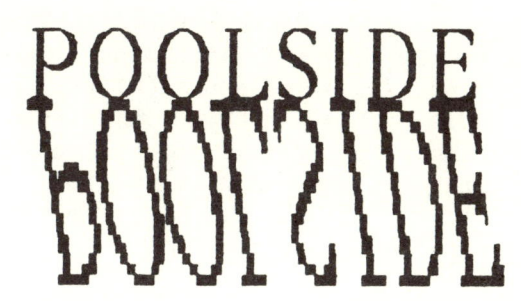

POOLSIDE

Fig. 4.20 A water reflection effect, making use of italic print, resizing and flipped.

This starts with the title typed in graphics text, using 24 point New York. The text is then retyped in 18 point New York italic. It has to be retyped because you *cannot* change the font of existing text when you are using graphics text. When you use normal text, you can highlight it and then change font, but no highlighting is possible with graphics text, and using a definition box does not have the same effect. With the new heading in 18 point italic, mainly because no 24 point italic is available on my disk, the heading is flipped vertically, then dragged under the main heading. The resizing command is then used to pull out the 'reflected' letters so that they fit exactly under the main letters, and also to distort them vertically. The step shape of the sloping letters then gives the impression of the effect of small waves on a reflection in water, which is what we want for this heading. It looks useful if you are selling swimming pool accessories.

Editing graphics text

Editing graphics text is not the same as editing normal text, as you might expect. Contrary to the advice of the manual, the delete-left key on the Amstrad will delete letters you have typed, but only when you have typed the letters in a straightforward sequence, not if you have been spacing letters with the mouse cursor. Once you have moved the cursor off the line, the delete-left key has no effect. The arrowed keys also have no effect on the graphics text cursor, so that if you see a mistake while you are typing, you can save a great deal of effort if you simply delete and correct at the time rather than waiting until later. Since you normally use graphics text for special effects, so that the amount of graphics text is small, this is not a great handicap.

When you have to carry out editing on text that has been entered, after the cursor has been moved about, things become more difficult. Apart from erasing and touching-up methods, dealt with in the following chapter, you are confined to a combination of definition box movement along with the Cut and Paste methods. Suppose, for example, that you have committed the error shown in Figure 4.21(a), with the word Caprice spelled with an S in place of a C. At the time when this was typed, of course, you could have used the delete-left key and retyped the letter, but we'll suppose that you did not notice and that the error has reached a later stage, perhaps when the user sees the proofs. How do you go about the replacement?

(1) With the word on screen, place a definition box around the unwanted letter S. Change to the hand pointer and drag the box with the letter S out of the way, as indicated in Figure 4.21(b).

(a) *Caprise*

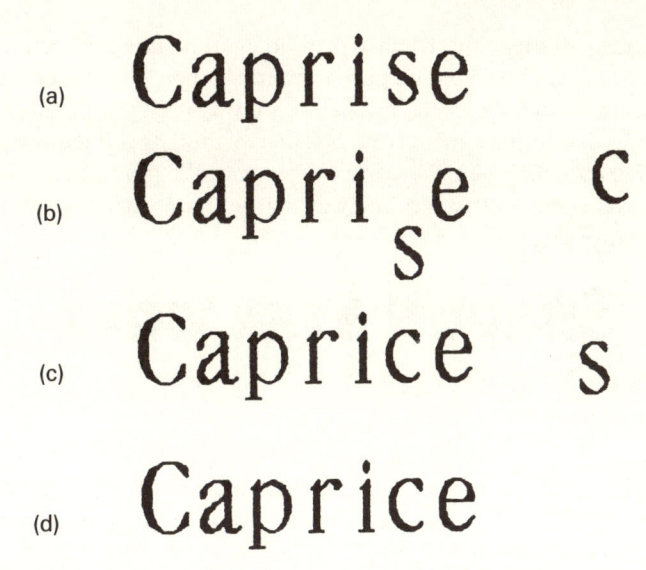

(b) *Capri e   c*
      s

(c) *Caprice   s*

(d) *Caprice*

Fig. 4.21 Stages in correction. (a) The original error. (b) The letter S being dragged out after surrounding it with a definition box. The correct letter C has been typed elsewhere. (c) The letter C dragged into place. (d) The letter S deleted by defining it and using Cut.

(2) Move the pointer aside, click on the graphics text A, and type the correct letter C, as also shown in Figure 4.21(b).
(3) Use the definition box tool to place a box around the letter C. Change to the hand pointer, and drag this letter into place, Figure 4.21(c).
(4) Put a definition box around the S and use the Art menu (or press DEL) to Cut this letter out, Figure 4.21(d). This leaves the word corrected.

You can deal with individual letters as indicated here, or groups of letters, whole words, phrases, whatever you like. Any form of typing error that can be dealt with by text editing can also be dealt with using graphics editing methods. Take, for example, the use of Cut and Paste. You can use Cut and Copy on any graphics text that is enclosed in a definition box, and you can then select graphics text and use Paste to restore the text at a different position. The position to which anything is pasted, however, is indicated by the hand pointer, and is the position of the top left hand corner of the definition box, rather then the first letter of the graphics text. Because of this, a pasted item usually needs to be finally positioned by means of the hand pointer, and it's much easier to run a definition box around the material and then use the hand pointer to move it in the first place. In this way, you can seen the text all the time you are working on it, a distinct advantage.

There is an important difference here between pure text and graphics text.

When you are working with ordinary text, you can highlight a section, and your highlighting can begin or end part-way along a line. This is not possible with graphics text, because the definition box is always of a rectangular shape, and so shifting words that spread from one line to another will require you to use more then one box. You also have to remember that you have to make space for graphics text, otherwise the text that you are inserting will merge with any existing text.

Shadow over sport

Fig. 4.22 Shadow style of text, produced by placing text and its duplicate copy close to each other.

This merging effect can be the basis of yet another way of drawing attention to your text, as Figure 4.22 indicates. In this example, the phrase has been printed in 'shadow' form as follows:

(1) Graphics text is selected and the phrase typed.
(2) The definition box is placed round the phrase.
(3) From the Art menu, select Cut.
(4) Now select graphics text again, and Paste from the Art menu.
(5) Paste in at the hand position (click mouse button) and move the copy so that it is just slightly displaced from the original. You can release the copy and look at the effect, then alter the position until you get what you want, before merging the images finally (by removing the definition box).

You can produce this effect using really large type, either 36-point or type that has been re-sized, giving interesting and eye-catching effects. As usual, you need to exercise your judgement to decide just what amount of shadowing produces the best results. Normal text often gives better shadow effects than bold and in fonts where the bold is of the same width as the normal type you can shadow normal with bold or bold with normal.

Another effect that is sometimes useful is the ability to work with individual letters, throwing a definition box around each and moving it or performing other work on it. Figure 4.23(a) shows a title which plays on the word 'ruins'. This can be more effectively done with Fleet Street Editor V.3.0, which allows for 90 degree rotation, so that the letters R and S can each be shown turned through 90 degrees rather than through 180 degrees. Another option is shown in Figure 4.23(b), in which each alternate letter is inverted. In each of the examples, a definition box has been put round individual letters so that the action of movement, flipping or inversion can be carried out on the individual letters in turn. Once again, this can give very striking results which should not be overdone.

(a) ꓤIN ꓛ

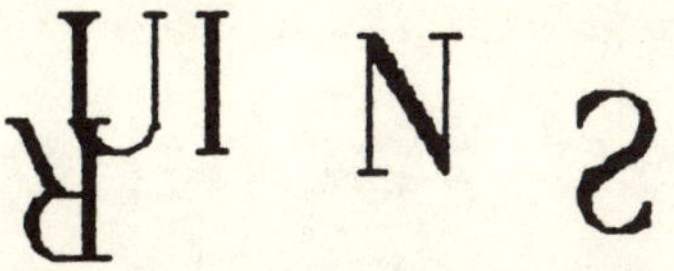

(b) A̶L̶T̶E̶R̶N̶A̶T̶E̶S̶

Fig. 4.23 Visual effects on words, flipping some letters (a) or inverting alternate letters (b).

Chapter Five
Advanced Techniques

Pencil and eraser

Any form of graphics, whether it be artwork or graphics text, can be worked on in a way that can be very creative and also very tedious, using the pencil and eraser tools. We have met the eraser briefly, but this is the chapter in which its potential, and that of the pencil, will be explored more fully. The pencil and the eraser are items 7 and 8 respectively, counting down the list of the side-tools. The pencil is represented by a rod, the eraser by a thick bar.

The action of the eraser is to place on screen as a pointer a fairly large rectangle. Anything within this rectangle will be erased when the mouse pointer is pressed, and if the rectangle is moved while the mouse button is depressed (half-click) then anything in the path of the rectangle will be erased. This offers considerable opportunity for doctoring your images; it also allows a lot of scope for making a complete mess of them, because there is no way of reducing the size of the rectangle that is being erased.

The pencil action can cause some head-scratching moments also. The action of the pencil is to draw a line or place a dot. When the pencil is selected, a pencil-like pointer appears and can be moved by the mouse. When the mouse button is depressed the pencil will leave a dot, and if the mouse is moved with the button held down, then the pencil maker will draw a line. This is your only method of drawing lines other than straight lines in Fleet Street Editor. The disconcerting thing about pencil, however, is that it can draw either in black or in white on your artwork. If your pencil has been drawing a line on the white screen area, then moving it into a black area will *not* cause it to draw a white line, but when the pencil is used (mouse button pressed) first on a black area, then it draws in white. Conversely, if you start the pencil drawing on a white area, it will continue drawing in black. You can sometimes find, then, that using the pencil to mend a piece of incorrectly erased material can cause further damage in the form of white lines in the black areas unless you are careful about where the pencil is positioned when you press the mouse button (or the F10 key).

One useful hint concerning the eraser has been noted earlier, but is worth repeating here. If you have to erase along a horizontal or a vertical line, do not rely on the steadiness of your hand on the mouse. Instead, position the eraser with the arrowed keys (or the mouse), and then press the F10 key (the equivalent of a half-click) and use a horizontal or vertical arrow key to move the eraser. Press the F10 key again when erasing is complete on that line. This technique allows you to get away with a lot of unsteady box drawing, as Figure 5.1 illustrates. This shows the stages in producing a work in alternate normal and inverse, as was also illustrated in Figure 4.23(b). As you can see, the inversion has used boxes of irregular size, but the use of the eraser moved in a perfectly straight line has tidied up the image.

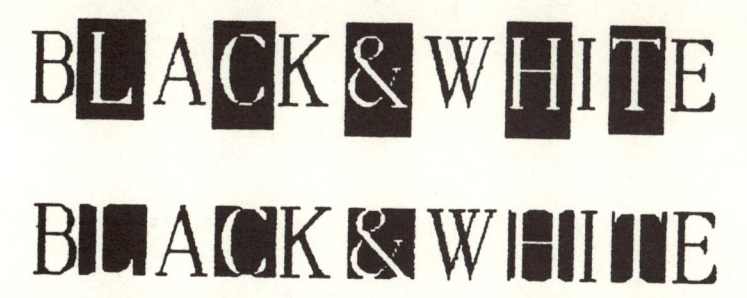

Fig. 5.1 How a set of reversed letters can be trimmed to look neater, using the eraser tool.

Another application is shown in Figure 5.2. The text in (a) has been typed and each alternate letter inverted, using the technique described in Chapter 4. Not shown in this illustration is the black bar which is then used as a top and bottom border. This is created by throwing a definition box around a piece of blank screen, making the box a wide shallow rectangle, and then inverting.

Fig. 5.2 Making and using bars. The black bars have been obtained by drawing a box and inverting it, then duplicating and dragging into place.

The black box is then duplicated, and one copy is dragged over the top of the letters, the other is dragged under. As you drag the black rectangles, the black portions above or below the letters show in white, but they revert to black when the dragging stops (when you release the mouse button). As an alternative, or if your mouse hand is shaky, you can use the F10/arrow key method to ensure perfect alignment. If the box is made wider than the phrase, you can now trim it with the eraser on each side, using the F10/arrow key method.

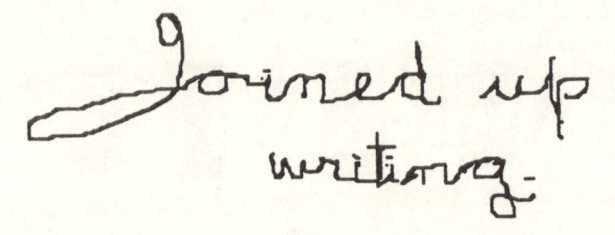

Fig. 5.3 Attempting to write using the mouse is hardly likely to win a calligraphy prize.

The point about the unsuitability of the mouse for artwork is brought out by Figure 5.3, which shows a *careful* attempt to write with the mouse and the pencil tool! No matter how good your handwriting is (and I have to admit that mine is unspeakable, something I blame on years of taking hasty notes) the results of writing with the mouse are never good. If you need your published work to incorporate joined-up writing, then it's better to use a font that consists of suitably shaped letters. Such a font is Bombay, one in the set of Decorative fonts sold on two $5\frac{1}{4}''$ disks (or one 3.5" disk) as an add-on the Fleet Street Editor. The Bombay font is illustrated in Figure 5.4, and it gives a good simulation of handwriting, though the lines are rather thicker than would be found in most handwriting. Bombay, however, is not a standard part of your Fleet Street Editor package (though the add-on fonts are reasonably priced and useful if you require such work), and the smallest size

Fig. 5.4 The Bombay font gives the appearance of writing, though the lines are rather thick.

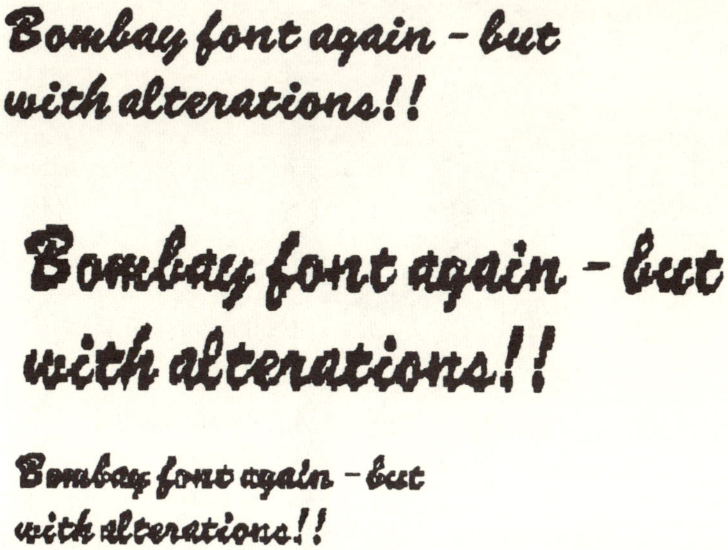

Advanced Techniques 93

*Bombay font again – but
with alterations!!*

*Bombay font again – but
with alterations!!*

*Bombay font again – but
with alterations!!*

Fig. 5.5 Bombay font can be resized, but the results are not good.

of Bombay is 24 point, as used here. Altering the scale of a piece of work in Bombay is not very satisfactory, as Figure 5.5 shows.

Using Magnify on graphics text

We have seen previously that letters of graphics text, when rescaled upwards, often look unsatisfactory, particularly because of the stepped appearance of sloping lines. This appearance can be improved, albeit at the expense of a lot of rather intensive effort. The principle is to magnify an unsatisfactory section so that the individual dots that make up the image can be edited. Because this requires so much effort, it should be confined to working on one graphics letter or one image, but if you have special requirements for a very large font, for example, you could make up an alphabet in which each letter had been worked on in this way and save this as a MAC file. A good point to remember is that you can often get better results by enlarging the image more than you need, editing it, and then resizing down to the size you want finally.

To illustrate the editing of resized material, put a graphics J on the screen in Helvetica 36 point and resize it to about 1.5″ high and 1″ wide. Remember to have the rulers showing on screen for any action like this, so that you can be sure of dimensions and not be caught out by the vertical distortion of the screen. Now when this resized J is printed, it looks rather like the one in

(a)

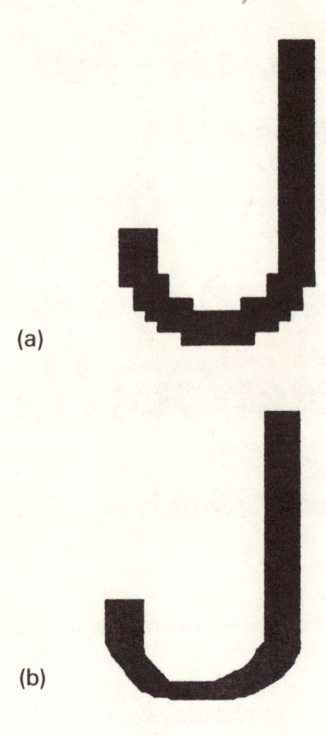

(b)

Fig. 5.6 Touching up artwork. (a) A resized letter J, showing the stepped appearance of the curves. This can be retouched (b) by using the Magnify command from the ART menu.

Figure 5.6(a). The curved portions are really steps, which in the smaller size look reasonably smooth, but which are far from smooth in the larger size. Now if we could whittle away at the edge of each step and fill in the depression, we could obtain a more rounded outline. The Magnify command from the Art menu allows this to be done, but it is by no means easy to maintain the thickness of a letter unless you can see a larger part of it. Figure 5.6(b) shows one effort in which the thickness of the letter has been reduced too much, but the smoother outline is well demonstrated.

To make use of the Magnify command:

(1) Select Art, and then Magnify.
(2) The screen will show your image, and the pointer will change to a small picture of a magnifying glass.
(3) Move the magnifying glass to where it is wanted, over a stepped portion of the image. Click the mouse button.
(4) You can now see a magnified image of part of the artwork, with a normal-

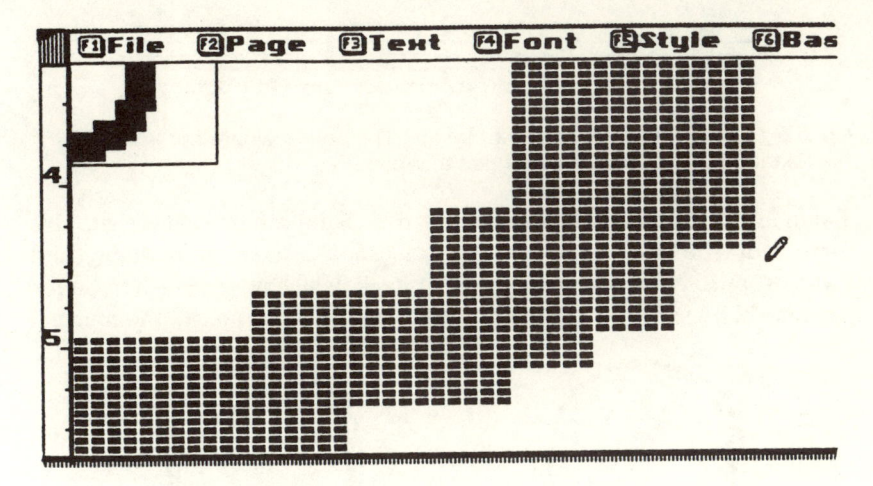

Fig. 5.7 The screen appearance during work on the J with Magnify. The main screen shows the detail, the corner image shows the piece in true size.

size view in the top left-hand corner. The pointer is now a pencil, see Figure 5.7.
(5) The magnified image is made up from little rectangles. These represent the dots on the screen, called pixels, that make up the image.
(6) By pressing the mouse button, you can change the pixel under the pencil-tip from white to black or from black to white.
(7) If you move the pencil to a group of pixels and hold the button down while moving the mouse, you will change the colour of each pixel. If you started in black pixels, you will only change black to white this way, not white to black. Conversely, if you started on white pixels, you will only change white to black, not black to white.
(8) If it all gets out of hand, pressing the Esc key will restore the original image.

The use of Magnify in this way allows a very considerable amount of control over graphics at the expense of a lot of effort. It is an ideal way of creating new artwork from established images, and it also allows the merging of images to be adjusted so that one image does not entirely obscure another. An example of this is shown in Figure 5.8, in which the words MUSIC TIME have been typed in graphics text, and then five lines (to represent a musical stave) drawn across the words. Normally, the points where the lines cross the letters would be black, but in this example the Magnify command has been used to change these crossing points to white, creating a more distinctive effect.

One of the main uses of Magnify, however, is in the editing of art images, so that if you want William Shakespeare smoking a pipe or to convert Mark

96 Desktop Publishing on a Shoestring

Fig. 5.8 Using Magnify to alter an image. The points where the lines and the text intersect have been changed to white.

Twain into Albert Einstein, then your artistic hand can have full reign. This sort of work, however, depends on the possession of some artistic ability, and I who dropped Art in favour of Ancient Greek (which was so much easier for a colour-blind left-hander) prefer not to alter the larger images too much.

Fig. 5.9 Changing the US style light bulb in the MAC file to a UK type of bayonet fitting.

Some images do need altering, however, and a prime example is the electric light bulb in the PERSONAL.MAC file. This is a US style bulb with an Edison screw fitting, and you might want to use the image to create a UK type of bayonet-fitting bulb. Figure 5.9 shows the original image on the left, and the edited image on the right. The steps were as follows.

(1) Get the bulb image from PERSONAL.MAC and create a duplicate. Working on a duplicate saves having to load PERSONAL.MAC in again if things go wrong.
(2) Use the Pencil to black out the white horizontal stripes of the screw thread. This is most easily done using the F10/arrow key method, remembering that if you start the pencil on a white area it will then write in black, but if you start on a black area the pencil will write in white.
(3) Use the Pencil now to fill in the serrations which suggest the screw thread at the side of the cap. Once again, start the pencil on a white area and work it up and down and to the side using F10 and the arrow keys.
(4) Now use the Magnify command to alter the bottom of the cap. Put in the two contacts, and then follow this with the side-pins. Watch the small-

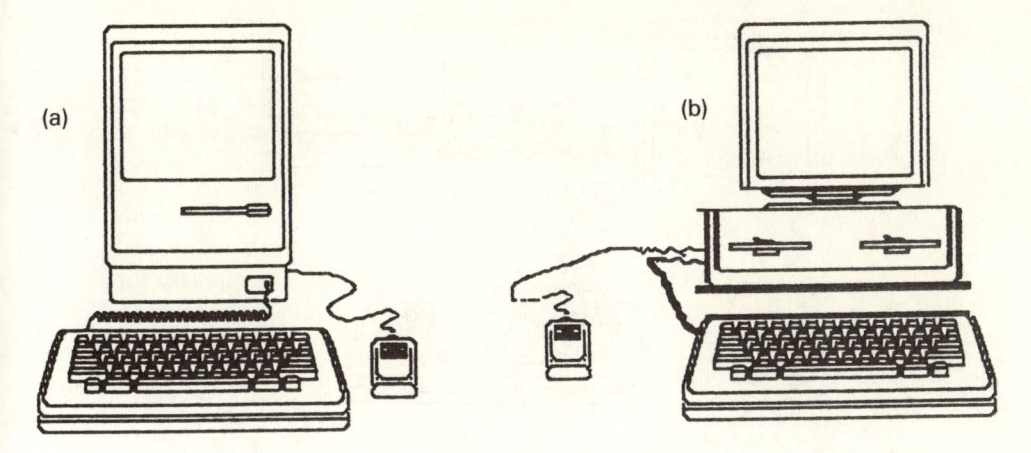

Fig. 5.10 The computer in the MAC file (a) is an Apple Macintosh. This can be converted with some editing into something like an Amstrad (b).

scale image closely as you work on the magnified view.

The resulting image is a much more acceptable bulb image for UK use, so you will probably want to keep this as one of your own images in an ART file ready for use in your graphics work.

If light bulb images are not suited to your work, how about a computer? The DESKITEM.MAC file contains a good computer image, but the computer is the Apple Macintosh, which looks nothing like any PC. The Apple Mac is a splendid machine, and is very popular for desktop publishing work, particularly in the USA where its price is reasonable. In the UK, the needs of business make it more difficult to sell computers that do not run the MS-DOS system and, for graphics purposes, the Atari ST is a fraction of the price of the Mac. You might therefore want to change this image to one that looks more like a computer you use, and in Figure 5.10 the change to an Amstrad style of PC machine is illustrated. This involves considerably more effort than was needed for the light bulb:

(1) The parts of the original image are separated, as indicated in Figure 5.11. This allows you to work on the portions separately. At this point, you can drag the mouse over to the left hand side, since it plugs into the Amstrad on the left hand side (American mice are right-handed, ours are left-handed).

(2) Start work on the screen, completing the outline, and adding the swivel-base. The main lines are drawn using the pencil, the fine detail that suggests the curvature of the base is added using Magnify.

(3) Now work on the disk-drive portion. Use Rescale first to widen this section, since the Mac image is narrower than that of a PC.

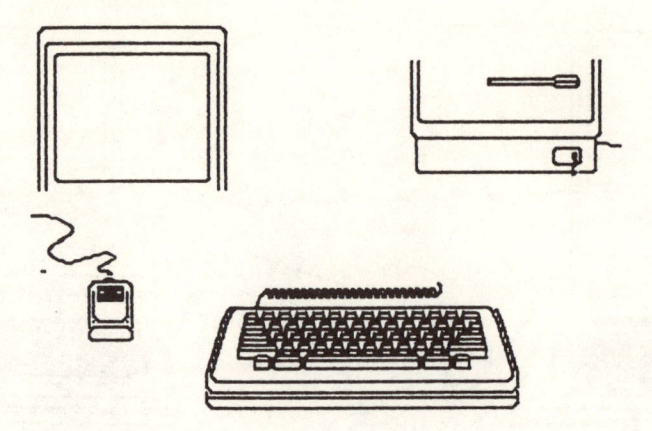

Fig. 5.11 The computer image taken apart by means of the definition box and the hand pointer.

(4) Draw a box around the disk slot, reduce its width, and use Magnify to change it to a type with a swing-lever fastener.
(5) Drag the disk drive as far to the right as possible, and use Duplicate to create another identical drive on the left. Position this drive correctly.
(6) Select the keyboard, and erase the connector cable.
(7) Now put the parts together, following Figure 5.10, and take a look. Remember to allow for the distorted nature of the screen image. You can use pencil to draw in connector cables between keyboard and main unit, and also complete the cable for the mouse.
(8) Now tidy up the image, using Magnify, until it looks suitable.

You can now save this ART image ready for use in any of your publications, such as business cards, headed paper, advertising flyers and the like. Adapting existing images like this may look like hard work, but it is very much easier than the effort that can be involved in creating an image from scratch. Even if your eye and hand are artistically inclined, there is a limit to what you can do with the mouse or with the F10/arrow keys. One aid is a light-pen, which enables you to 'draw' on the screen with a pen-shaped device which will leave dots and lines on the screen as you draw. If you can draw on a blackboard, then you can probably do a good job with a light pen, and a suitable low-cost pen, along with the necessary software, is supplied by The Electric Studio Products Ltd whose address is shown in Appendix C. Note that the fitting of the light-pen requires removing covers from the computer and you should not attempt it if you have never opened the box before. If you have some hardware experience (and if the metal cover over the circuit board of your Amstrad PC is cut in the correct place!) then the fitting is not difficult. If you have absolutely no experience of fitting devices inside the computer, get

Advanced Techniques 99

an experienced dealer to do the fitting.

Though it's rather out of place in a book that deals with desktop publishing on the proverbial shoestring, The Electric Studio Products also markets a complete video camera outfit at a price that is quite astonishingly low, comparable with the price of a dot-matrix printer. The camera allows you to capture any image, of real objects, posters, book illustrations (remember that those are subject to copyright) or any other source. This is by far the easiest way into graphics images for the non-artistic. The alternative is any of the numerous drawing/painting packages of software for the PC, though personally I would not be particularly interested in any package that did not use a light-pen.

Images and messages

Several of the images in your graphics library are tailor-made for carrying messages typed in graphics text. Figure 5.12 shows one of the screen images from the DISPLAY.MAC collection used to show an advertising message. The message is typed using graphics text, which allows each line or block of text to be positioned where you want it within the display area. Three sizes of the New York font have been used here, underlined by a box drawn with the box side-tool.

Fig. 5.12 Graphics text on a graphics image, useful for advertising work.

As often happens, the screen image cannot be extracted from the MAC file without taking parts of other images, and these should be deleted, using the eraser tool. Remember that if your message is longer (a message that is too long will not be read) you can use the Resize command of the Art menu to enlarge the area. In an image like this, you need not be too pedantic about preserving proportions, so that you can make the screen fit the words if you feel so inclined. You could even type the words using normal text methods (not using Graphics text) and then move the screen image on to the words. Working this this allows you to manipulate the projector-screen image as much as you like, because the graphics manipulation will not interfere with the text. If you use Graphics text then once you shift the definition box away from the projector screen (after placing it on the words, or the words on the screen) then you have merged the images, and any text editing will then be harder work.

Figure 5.13 shows another display image, with added messages this time. The image is extracted from DISPLAYS.MAC as before, and tidied up to remove traces of other images. The words in the display frame are put in using Geneva bold, and the wording underneath is put in with New York, using 24 point and 14 point sizes. The display wording needs little explanation, but the external words have involved some subterfuge. When you type across a black area, such as the skirt in this image, and then delete, you can see the words appear in inverse video. This tempts you to think that the final image will show this, but it does not. You have then two options. The one used here is to delete the black of the skirt, leaving only the outline, in the places where the

Fig. 5.13 Another way of using an image, with text both in the frame and across the image.

words will cross. The alternative is to type the parts of the words that will be concealed at a different part of the screen, put a definition box around them, and then invert. They can then be moved into place, and any overlapping black deleted or edited with the Magnify command. This requires rather more patience, but can look very effective.

Fig. 5.14 A message in a bubble. The original graphics image has been heavily worked on, and the bubble added. The text is graphics text.

Another way of creating messages from images is to show a character speaking in the time-honoured convention of the comic-strips, the bubble. Figure 5.14 shows such a message, converted from the singer image in the PERSONAL.MAC file. The stages in the preparation of this were:

(1) The singer image was put into ART file form, removing bits of other images.
(2) The eraser was used to remove the microphone and the musical notes, then the pencil was used to black out the gaps. The outline was then cleaned up with the eraser.
(3) A blank rectangle was outlined with the definition box, and then inverted to make it a black box. This was then dragged alongside the image on the

right hand side. The edges were lined up with those of the original image, using the eraser.
(4) The bubble was drawn roughly with the pencil and its inner area cleared with the eraser.
(5) The details of the bubble were then edited, using Magnify. In particular, the black-on-white parts were put in, and the rough edges of the pencilled outline were smoothed. Main attention was to the point where the bubble leaves the mouth.
(6) The wording was then put in place using Graphics text in the usual way.

The use of bubbles for messages is sometimes more effective than the use of strictly rectangular panels, and in this example you have many options that you can experiment with. The original image could, for example, be inverted or resized, and you could have used Duplicate and Horizontal flip to make two faces looking at each other and issuing a joint bubble. If you have to put in copy like 'Here's something to sing about', then this type of image can be very useful.

Decorated lettering

The use of decorated lettering is definitely an item of which a little goes a long way, but which can be useful at times. Figure 5.15 shows an advertising layout which looks appropriate for a garden centre. The flowery letters are taken from FRENCH.MAC, a set of embellished letters called French Manuscript.

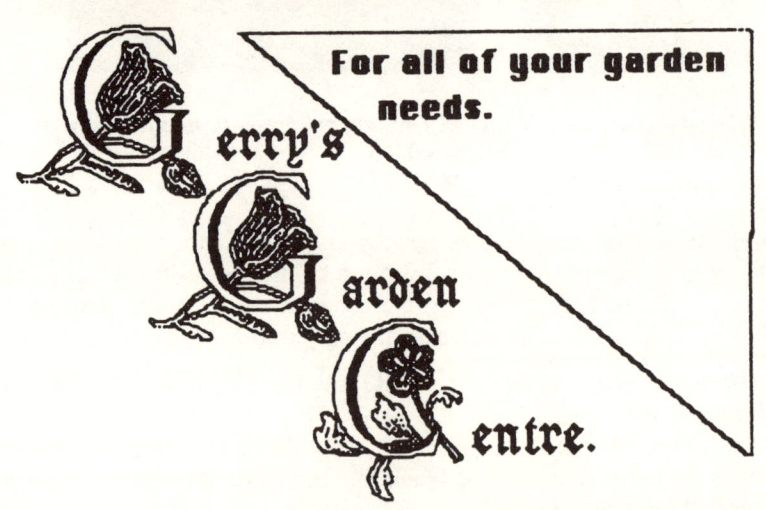

Fig. 5.15 Using decorated letters from the FRENCH.MAC set. These are appropriate to this kind of message.

Advanced Techniques **103**

In this example, the letters have been used unchanged, but you have, of course, the usual options to invert, resize or edit. The FRENCH.MAC page also contains spare flowers and leaves which you can add in and then drag around to add to the ornamental effect. Your efforts are considerably assisted in V.3.0 of Fleet Street Editor, which allows you to turn such images by 90 degrees.

Fig. 5.16 Stencil letters applied against an appropriate background.

There is also a set of stencilled lettering available, and this can be used to effect to indicate a rush job, emergency or urgency generally. The stencil letters are available horizontal or at an angle, so that you can obtain either pattern. Like the use of the French Manuscript letters, stencil needs to be used sparingly, and Figure 5.16 shows a typical application. The whole alphabet has been taken into an ART file – note that this means that you have to put a definition box around all the letters and then save as an ART file. Fleet Street Editor will not allow you to convert a MAC file to an ART file other than by the use of a definition box, even if this means placing a definition box around the whole of a page.

A problem can occur when you are picking out letters from a set like this. In the course of enclosing a wanted letter by a definition box, you are likely to enclose part of another letter – this is almost inevitable when you are picking out the sloping letters, because the definition box is always rectangular. The required letter can, of course, be cleaned up with the eraser, but you might need the letter that has been damaged in the move. There are several options for this:

(1) Put a small definition box around the part of the letter that has been removed, and drag it back again. This is by far the best method, as it ensures that the letter reverts to its shape quickly and easily.
(2) Erase all the remaining letters (use definition box and Cut) and load in the page again.
(3) Try to mend the letter with the pencil, eraser and Magnify command.

The use of these letterings is not something that can give you quick results, and you might prefer to use the additional fonts that you can buy for Fleet Street Editor, the Decorative fonts and the Executive fonts. These are all available in the larger point sizes only, as all are intended for display work.

Making logos

A logo is often a desirable part of any business card or headed notepaper. In the past, the creation of a logo was a time-consuming and labour-intensive task, and once a logo had been created the user tended to be stuck with it. If you can create your logo using desktop publishing techniques, the cost and time will both be greatly reduced, and you have the chance to edit the logo as much as you like. If you find that your chosen logo looks too large on a business card, then you can reduce the size. Conversely, if you find that your logo looks too small on headed notepaper, then it can be enlarged. If enlargement makes the image look too 'stepped' then the use of Magnify can smooth the shape until it is acceptable.

What you use for a logo is very much up to your own inventiveness, together with the possible use of images taken from the MAC files. These, as you know by now, do not need to be complete images, and they can also be edited to a considerable extent. As an example, we shall show how a logo for an imaginary firm, Crosstone Radio, might be developed and used on business cards and headed paper. We shall assume that the MD would like a logo that looks like a radio with music coming out of it, and that a CR letters motif is needed to emphasise the name. The business cards will be of the standard 3.5″ × 2″ size, and the notepaper will be A4, which is about 8.3″ × 11.7″. This last size is not quite so relevant, because we need only ensure that any heading will not overlap the paper, nor take up too much depth.

The first part concerns the logo, and Figure 5.17 shows a first effort at this. The framework is intended to show the final size of a business card, and will

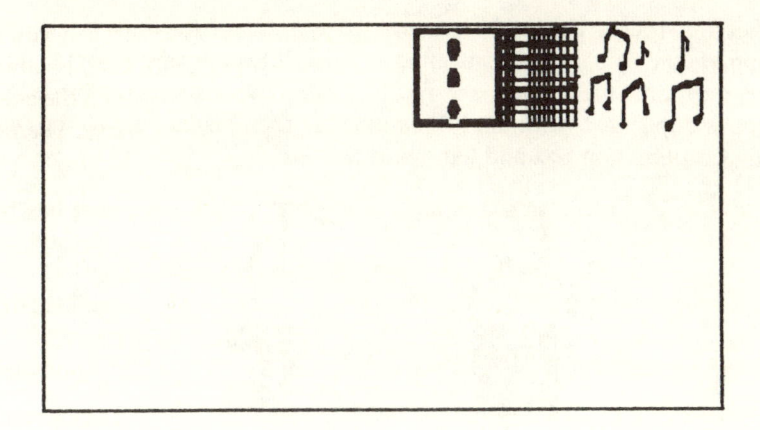

Fig. 5.17 A first attempt at creating a logo to order.

be erased when the work is done. The radio image has been assembled, Frankenstein-like, from various bits and pieces, and the musical notes have also been obtained from the DINGBATS.MAC file. Printing a first trial, using draft print, shows an unexpected problem – 3.5″ on the screen rulers is closer to 3″ on the actual paper, so that we have to expand the width of the framework in order to get the proportions correct. The first effort is amended, the musical notes tidied up, and various adjustments made.

Now how did we get to that stage? The effect of the radio grille has been brought from DINGBATS.MAC along with the musical notes, shown in Figure 5.18. The sizes of the notes have been reduced because they looked out of proportion, and some time has been spent in using Magnify to mend the fractures caused by the reduction in size. The grille image has also been reduced – it was too deep, even allowing for the screen distortion, and the new size looks as if it will give a more square shape when reduced. The rest of the radio box shape has been drawn in using the straight-line drawing tool, and this also has been tidied up using Magnify to sort out places where lines touch

Fig. 5.18 The separate parts of the logo, showing the 'grille' and the musical notes, along with the start of the control knobs.

or fail to to touch. The knobs have started as a square drawn with the pencil. Using Magnify pulls the square out to a rectangle to compensate for the screen distortion, and the corners are rounded off. The first reasonable-looking shape is duplicated twice, and the knobs are then pulled over to the radio, using the definition box and hand pointer.

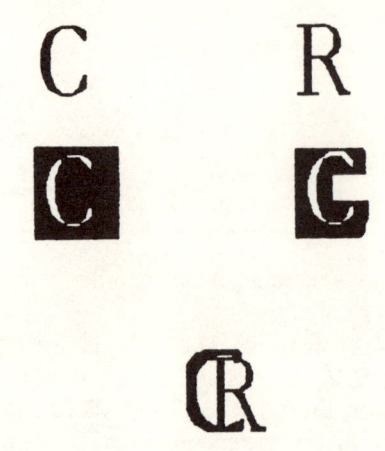

C R

C C

CR

Fig. 5.19 Working with letter patterns to produce a monogram. Obviously, this would require considerable retouching before it could be considered suitable.

The next part requires text to be inserted. This calls for a pair of initials, done in some fancy style, and so this is the next part to be designed. Figure 5.19 shows the steps in this design, Mark-1 version. The two letters are typed, using 36 point New York. The C is inverted, then the black centre removed, using the eraser to start with and then Magnify. The shape is then pulled over the R, and the black at the left side of the C is then eaten away, using the eraser and Magnify. This is printed in smoothed form, and taken to the customer. It's unsatisfactory, because the C is the important part, and he wants a large C with a smaller R. Grumbling that he might have said so in the first place, you start again.

This time, Figure 5.20, you start with 36 point Helvetica letters, and you enlarge the C, then smooth it with Magnify. The R is pulled across and fits gratifyingly well into the C. A little more adjustment, and extending the serifs (the feet) of the R follows to give the letter combination shown. This one is better liked, though the C still looks irregular.

The next step is to print a trial card, as in Figure 5.21. Notice that the shape of the card in print is so different from that on the screen that it's difficult to feel that you are getting things right. The Show Page command, however, will give you some idea of what the final effort will look like, from the point of

C R
C
R

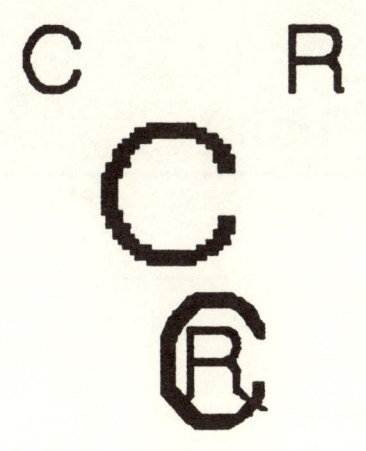

Fig. 5.20 Another form of monogram, using resizing and Magnify. This also requires retouching.

view of proportions. The shape of the card on the screen leads you to believe that you can print a lot more lines of type than are actually possible.

What can we learn from all this? One point is that design on paper, showing relative sizes, is vitally important, because it can save a lot of trial printing. The second is that where lettering is concerned, the less you have to rework it (resizing and reshaping) the better. If you need fancy lettering, then a disk of extra fonts is very much better than a lot of working over an enlarged image. The Executive and Decorative fonts of Fleet Street Editor come in sizes that for some fonts go up to 72 point, 1" size, and the choice that is available should cope with just about anything that can be required of

Crosstone Radio –
Radio & Audio Specialists

Tony Pachelbel-Canon

Fig. 5.21 A trial print of a business card using the pattern developed in the previous illustrations, before retouching.

Crosstone Radio
Radio & Audio

Stonedeaf House,
Postle Way,
Fillingside, Twits.

Date:

Fig. 5.22 Paper heading making use of the same patterns, before retouching.

desktop publishing on a shoestring. The simpler the logo you use, the better, because elaborate designs do not usually reproduce well, and cause a lot of problems if you want them in several different sizes. Before making a judgement on a logo, look at it on paper, preferably showing it in the correct context and size.

Now what might we offer for a headed paper? Figure 5.22 is a reduced scale version of what might be acceptable. The radio design is slightly smaller on this scale because whereas the business card could be shown full-size on a page in the book, the A4 paper size cannot, so that it appears in reduced form here. The title appears with first letters in 36 point Helvetica, and the remainder in 24 point. The side information is in 18 point of the same font, and a thick line separated this part from the address, which is in 12 point Geneva. This space would also normally carry a telephone number, and is separated in turn from the text which will follow it by another line, thin this time.

If you have been trying out these actions for yourself, you will realise by now that the creation of any kind of documentation other than the simplest newsletter involves a considerable amount of work, though not nearly as much as would be needed by older methods. One point is that the location of images can take a lot of effort. You can make some of this work easier by using the Move in Steps command of the Page menu. The default step size is 0.25″, and this means that when, for example, you pull a graphics shape across the screen, the movement will be in steps of 0.25″ instead of continuously (or, to be more precise, in steps of one pixel). Movement in steps can be useful for alignment, and its greatest advantage is that the grid lines that are drawn to indicate the step size extend beyond the present screen image. In other words, if you have a piece of text starting at the fourth vertical line from the left hand side at the top of a page, then this vertical can still be seen and used as a guide at the bottom of the page when the top is well out of sight owing to the unequal horizontal and vertical dimensions of the screen image.

The grid that is laid on to the screen by the Move in steps command is also useful for dimension checking. If, for example, you have drawn on to the

Advanced Techniques

screen an object that should be square or circular, you know that it needs to be stretched out vertically in order to look correct on the paper. You can use Move in steps both in the stretching process (which is therefore much quicker) and for checking that the number of grid lines in each direction is equal.

Advertising flyers

If your desktop publishing work requires the construction of advertising flyers, single sheets that are handed out or enclosed in newspapers or magazines, then you will probably need to use the larger fonts from the add-on collection. The Executive fonts will probably be more useful for these purposes than the Decorative fonts, though both can be useful. The executive font range consists of seven, all of which are available in a restricted range of large sizes, and in normal and italic only, no bold.

Name	Point range
Boston	24 to 48
Calgary	36 and 48
Inverness	24 to 48
Oxford	24 to 48
Plymouth	24 to 48
Quebec	48 and 72
Sydney	24 and 36

Figure 5.23 demonstrates these fonts, each in the smallest size of normal style, so that you can see the distinctive shapes. The phrase that is being typed is the start of the 'quick brown fox jumped over the lazy dog' which uses each letter of the alphabet, but you can see that in the limited width that is permitted for an illustration, some of these fonts do not get very far with this phrase in one line. The Quebec is useful if you have restricted line space and need to get a message over in large print. All of these fonts are very legible, though the Calgary looks rather stepped when printed on a dot-matrix machine as this example was. This can suggest a magnified image of typing that can be useful for some purposes. The shoestring operator using a 9-pin dot-matrix printer should go as far as possible for fonts that use straight lines rather than curves, because these always reproduce better.

Boston quick brown

Calgary quick

Inverness quick brown

Oxford quick brown

Plymouth quick

Quebec quick brown

Sydney quick

Fig. 5.23 The Executive fonts of Fleet Street Editor, which are an optional extra, on two 5¼" disks or one 3.5" disk.

Some work may require the decorative fonts, and once again you can buy a collection of such fonts as an extra. The range is:

Name	Sizes	Styles
Aberdeen	24 to 48	Normal only
Bermuda	36 and 48	Normal and italic
Bombay	24 to 72	Normal only
Canterbury	36	Normal, italic, shadow
Fargo	48	Normal and italic
Heidelberg	36 and 48	Normal only
Nairobi	36 and 48	Normal only
Seville	24 to 48	Normal only
Vegas	48 and 72	Normal only

and Figure 5.24 shows this set, once again printing as much of the quick brown fox as possible and all in the smallest sizes available which in some

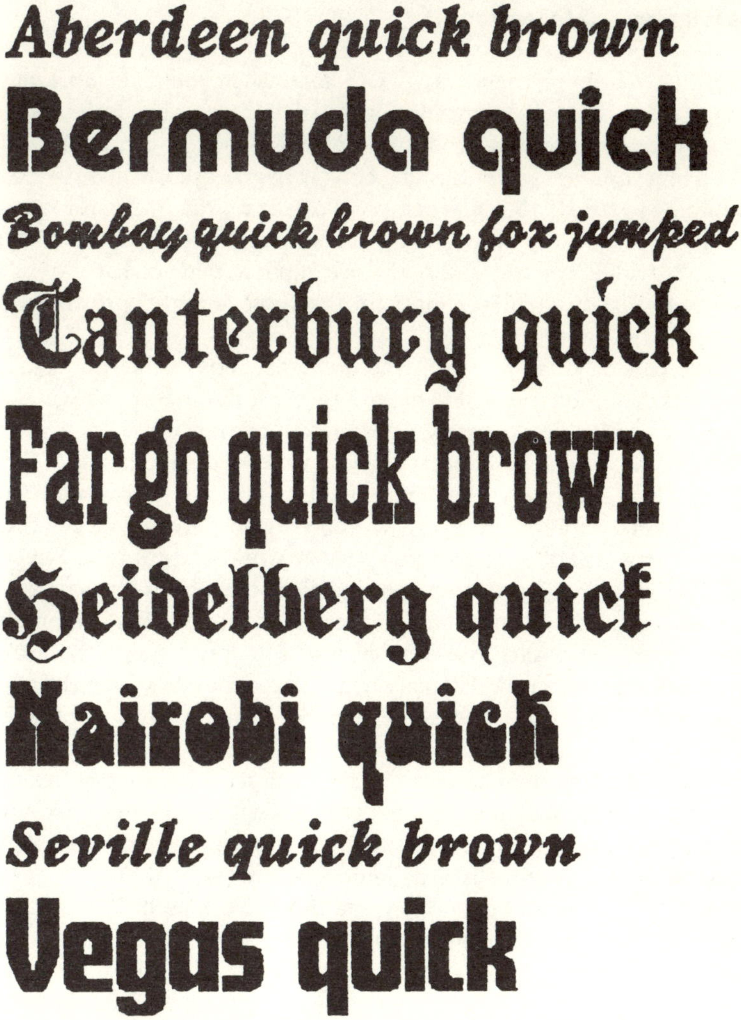

Advanced Techniques **111**

Aberdeen quick brown

Bermuda quick

Bombay quick brown fox jumped

Canterbury quick

Fargo quick brown

Heidelberg quick

Nairobi quick

Seville quick brown

Vegas quick

Fig. 5.24 The Decorative fonts of Fleet Street Editor, also extras.

cases are the only sizes. Decorative fonts need rather more consideration than the Executive fonts, because not everyone can read some of the more grotesque varieties, like Heidelberg (that k looks too much like a t). You can use fonts like this for a heading in an advertisement, but for large text, you would be better with an Executive font, though Fargo and Vegas are not too tiring on the eye. If you need smaller sizes, then you can make use of the normal fonts such as Geneva, New York and so on.

Leaving space for artwork

At times, you do not have artwork to hand when you make up a page. This applies particularly to magazine and newsletter work, in which you might be waiting for contributions from other people. Also, in such work, you might be mixing your desktop publishing copy with artwork which is pasted in after trimming to size. If your reprographics can cope, you might, for example, be using photos pasted on to desktop publishing sheets to create your master copy. Providing you can specify the size of photo that you can use (or the size you trim to), you can make space for the photos or other artwork while you compose the page.

This can be done by using PictureWrap. You create on your page a graphics definition frame, and move it to where the artwork will go. Since this is a piece of graphics, you have freedom to move it where you want, and with PictureWrap turned on, the text will wrap itself around one side of the frame. When the page is printed, the space that is to be occupied by the artwork will be left blank, with the text neatly wrapped against it, and you can then paste in your artwork. If, of course, you have artwork ready in Fleet Street Editor ART form, then the art can be put in before the page is printed.

This becomes very much more difficult if you need to put in more than one such illustration. Probably the easiest way is to draw a box of the correct size, put a definition box round it, place it, and wrap your text. Whenever you have passed this point, make another box, place a definition frame round it, move it to its place, and keep on typing the text – all the time with PictureWrap switched on. What you have to be careful about is having pictures too close to each other. If, of course, they are side by side, you can put a definition box around both, and wrap text around, but you cannot wrap text around an illustration unless there is a definition box around it, and the text wraps around the definition box, not around the artwork itself. If you keep to one such illustration per page, life is much simpler, but if you need more than one, make sure that a few lines of text separate them. You can, of course, ignore PictureWrap altogether, and prepare as many picture spaces as you like by working on the baselines, and this is the best method if you need to reserve a lot of spaces.

Using SNAPSHOT and SNAP2ART

You probably have various programs that generate screen displays. On the business side, programs like Ability, Lotus 1-2-3 and many others will generate displays of graphs, bar charts, pie diagrams and the like, from statistics fed into the program. In addition, you will have the normal display of items like spreadsheets, database entry forms and other (mainly text) patterns. If you are interested in graphics patterns, there are many programs, some of CAD (Computer-aided design) standard that allow you to create graphics with your PC, and such packages are also available on other computers. The Atari ST, in particular, being so well suited for graphics work, has available many drawing and painting packages. The Amstrad PC machine comes with the Basic-2 language which has extensive graphics capabilities, and which can be used to create, for example, circles of various sizes and styles to add to your art collection.

Some of these displays can be transferred to a Fleet Street Editor page, but you do not need to have Fleet Street Editor loaded or working at the time. The action is carried out by two supplementary programs that are on your Master disk, SNAPSHOT and SNAP2ART. The action of these, however, requires some explanation if you are to get the best out of them, and you also need to know which programs cannot make use of them. SNAPSHOT is a program that is memory resident, meaning that once you load it into the memory, it lurks there ready to be used on whatever program is running at the time. You can load in SNAPSHOT by typing its name in the usual way, with the program on the currently used disk or in a directory of the hard disk that is available at the time. One point that needs watching is that SNAPSHOT should be loaded once in each session, and if you want to make extensive use of SNAPSHOT you should place the command SNAPSHOT on your AUTOEXEC.BAT file, making sure that the SNAPSHOT program is on the same disk. What you must *not* do is to put SNAPSHOT on a batch file that calls up Fleet Street Editor (or any other program), because if you change from one program to another and back again, you could be loading SNAPSHOT more than once. This means that you will have more than one copy in the memory, since it loads into a different part of the memory each time, and you will eventually start to get 'Out of Memory' notices as you use your programs.

SNAPSHOT operates by the same method as the Print Screen action of the PC – you press the SHIFT and PrtSc keys. If you load SNAPSHOT manually, you can specify other keys to bring it into action, and this can be useful if you want to be able to use the PrtSc keys for something else. Do not think, however, that shifting the action to another key will still allow you to make use of the normal PrtSc action. For most purposes, however, the SNAPSHOT action is preferable in any case because it takes less time, and the final printing can be of much better quality.

SNAPSHOT cannot always be used, and its presence will sometimes interfere with other programs. You might, for example, use the Ability all-in-one business program and wish to make a snapshot of the screen to use with Fleet Street Editor. Ability has, however, its own SNAPSHOT action, and this overrides the Fleet Street Editor one so that you cannot get any action when you press the Shift-PrtSc keys. It is possible that a few programs might

114   Desktop Publishing on a Shoestring

not display correctly when SNAPSHOT is present.

When SNAPSHOT acts, it copies the screen data to the memory, not to a file. This implies that SNAPSHOT is ephemeral, and its action will be lost when the machine is switched off. To make a permanent file out of a SNAPSHOT, you need to use its 'other half', the SNAP2ART program, and the sequence of action is as follows:

(1) Make sure that SNAPSHOT has been loaded, either by the AUTO-EXEC.BAT file or by a direct command. We'll assume that you are using the straightforward PrtSc key method.
(2) Start using the program from which you want to take a screen image.
(3) When the image that you want is on screen, press the SHIFT-PrtSc keys together. If you have the volume control turned on, you will hear a beep to indicate a successful snap.
(4) You can take only one snap like this in a session, and to convert it into permanent form you need to use the SNAP2ART program. If you make a second snapshot at this point, only the second will be used.
(5) Leave the program which has provided the graphics or other screen display that you have captured.
(6) Use the SNAP2ART program to make an ART file. If you want this to be called DISPLAY, for example, use the command:

   SNAP2ART DISPLAY

   – making sure that you have the SNAP2ART program on the drive or directory that you are using.
(7) You should see on the screen the image that you have captured, along with a menu that allows you to adjust the picture starting at the top left or bottom right portions. You can then use the E key to confirm that you want the image converted into an ART file, or the Q key to quit so that you can make another choice of image to snap.
(8) You should now have the file DISPLAY.ART on your disk, and you can read this into Fleet Street Editor like any other ART file.

In general, SNAPSHOT works best on programs that generate graphics screens and which have no alternative snapshot system built into them. If a program incorporates the same type of action, using the Shift-PrtSc keys, then this will always override your use of SNAPSHOT, and the alternative method of loading SNAPSHOT (using SNAPSHOT K) will not help. You can, however, use SNAPSHOT on the screens that Fleet Street Editor itself creates (though not on the SNAP2ART screen itself) and with any program on which the Shift-PrtSc keys have their normal effect when SNAPSHOT is not in use.

Chapter Six
Final Words

Laser fonts

With your copy of Fleet Street Editor, you have a disk of Laser Support programs, and in both disk versions, this is a complete disk that contains two files called APLASER.FNT and HPLASER.FNT. These disks contain fonts that are particularly well suited to laser printers, but you can use these fonts on a dot-matrix printer if you wish. One of the fonts in the APLASER.FNT set is Times which is a very comprehensive font for newspaper work, and you might want to try it out for your own newsletter.

This is Times Roman (Normal) in 12-point, one of the laser fonts in the APLASER.FNT file on your Laser support disk. This font exists in a very large range of sizes, and in this demonstration we can show the 10-point and also the very tiny 9-point sizes that exist in Times. These very small sizes do not reproduce well on a dot-matrix printer.

Fig. 6.1 The Times font, which is on the laser support disk in the APLASER.FNT file.

The Times font of Fleet Street Editor is illustrated in Figure 6.1, and you can see that it looks distorted and rather smaller in 12 point size than your other fonts do in the same point size. The clarity of the type on a dot-matrix printer is not particularly good, as the illustration shows, particularly in the smaller sizes, and you might find that you want to use 14 point. There are normal (known as Roman), bold, italic and bold-italic styles in Times for most sizes, so that this font offers an enormous variety. Even the 18 point is not an excessively large type size, but the 14 point looks reasonable on a page, as Figure 6.2 shows. Your biggest font range, after Times, is for Helvetica which is particularly rich in the smaller sizes, offering 7, 9, 10, 12, and 14 in

This is Times 14-point normal (Roman), which looks very narrow on screen but prints well. Your typing needs to be slow to allow this to be input directly, but you can, of course, place the print in from a file.

Fig. 6.2 Times Roman in 14 point size.

its range of smaller sizes, with bold, italic and bold-italic available in addition to normal in many sizes. There are only a few of the Helvetica sizes on your MASTER.FNT file as you receive it, and you might want to extend the range by drawing from the APLASER.FNT file. These laser printer files are transferred exactly like any other extra fonts, by using FONTMOVE. Remember that the number of fonts that you can have at any one time in your MASTER.FNT file is limited, even if you use a hard disk. Figure 6.3 shows some of the smaller Helvetica options from 14 point downwards. The printing quality with a dot matrix printer is not as good as with the Geneva and New York fonts.

You have to remember that the laser fonts – Postscript Helvetica, Postscript Times, Postscript Courier, HP Lineprinter, HP Courier and HP Times Roman – are designed to be used with a laser printer. As printed by dot-

Helvetica in 14-point looks like this, and you have a very wide choice of sizes in this face also. We can use 12-point, as in this sentence. Also available is 10-point, this one, and even the remarkably tiny 7-point that you might use for the important get-out clauses on contracts!

Fig. 6.3 The Helvetica laser font, which comes in a very large range of sizes also.

matrix, therefore, they look rather distorted and the size is incorrect – as Figures 6.1, 6.2 and 6.3 show. These typefaces will look excellent, however, when printed by a laser printer – in particular the Apple or Hewlett-Packard for which they were designed. The fonts that you would normally use with a dot-matrix printer, however, will not necessarily appear in a much higher quality if printed by one of the lower cost laser printers. This is because these lower price laser printers emulate the action of other printers such as the Epson, though there is a noticeable advantage for graphics work because most laser printers are capable of printing 300 dots per inch and of course the speed of printing is much higher.

This month's Wines....

Macon Blanc 1986	£4.85
Pouilly Fuisse	£8.75
Niersteiner '85	£6.22
Piesporter '86	£3.25
Mouton Cadet '85	£4.66
Chateau LaTour '85	£9.65

Fig. 6.4 An example of the result you can obtain using an Apple LaserWriter and laser fonts.

Figure 6.4 shows the result that can be obtained using an Apple LaserWriter and laser fonts. The dot-matrix result was shown previously as Figure 4.1 on page 66.

Absent friends

Fleet Street Editor contains a large number of facilities, certainly more than enough for the desktop publisher working on a shoestring, but there are a few actions that are *not* provided which nevertheless you ought to know about. The first of these concerns *tracking* and *kerning*. These words describe adjustments to the spacings between letters within words, and some of the expensive desktop publishing packages permit these adjustments to be done automatically (not always a good thing) or manually. Tracking means moving letters slightly further apart, and kerning means moving them together, and the purpose of these actions is to get print looking better. To anyone who has never dabbled with print, these adjustments look pointless, and you might find that some automatically kerned material from a desktop publishing package looks rather less readable than the same material left to its own devices. This is an excellent argument for leaving these adjustments out of Fleet Street Editor, because unless kerning and tracking are done manually by someone with a good eye for print quality and considerable experience, they are best left undone.

Widows and clubs (or 'orphans' as they are known in software houses) are quite another matter. When your text takes more than one page, it is possible to have one line of a paragraph on one page, and the rest on another. You might, for example, have the first line of a paragraph on the end of a page (a club line), or the last, short, line at the start of a page (a widow), and these detached lines, the widows and clubs, look untidy. Users of some word processors, notably LocoScript, will have used automatic prevention of widows and clubs (or 'orphans'), and on most other word processors it is possible to specify with a command placed in the text (an embedded command) that a new paragraph will have to take a new page if only one line can be fitted on the existing page. There is no such provision in Fleet Street Editor, however, and you will have to guard against the untidy appearance of widows and clubs for yourself, looking carefully at each page of your text for badly-split paragraphs.

Purpose and style

By the time you read this portion of this book, you should be equipped technically to undertake any kind of desktop publishing with Fleet Street Editor. Being technically equipped, however, does not mean that you can make a pleasing job of the process. A glance at some computing magazines will reveal advertisements which have been created using desktop publishing by users with an excellent technical grasp of the hardware and the software. They show the use of almost every font and every variation of size and style but they look as out of place among professionally designed typeset work as an abacus at a computer show. All the technical wizardry in the world cannot prevent work looking amateurish if it is not accompanied by some feeling for what the final product looks like. Excessive use of effects in print is the equivalent of 'go-faster' stripes (also known as 'ape-tape') on cars. The purpose of your publishing efforts is to call attention to a text message, and if the message is confusing to the eye it will not reach the parts that count, which are the parts that think.

Your task, then, is to design your documents. This has to be done with the computer switched off, because there's nothing quite so seductive as a blank screen which can be written on with a variety of fonts. The design of your publications has to be done on the medium that they will eventually appear on, paper. If you are working with items like business cards which must contain their information within a small and fixed format, then you will find it useful to use squared paper. Most graph paper nowadays is scaled in cm and mm, which is not really useful for print design, but with some perseverance you can still find paper that is scaled in $\frac{1}{10}''$ squares. Filofax owners can buy a sheet called Quadrille which is scaled in various fractions of an inch, and this is ideal for laying out print designs whether you own a Filofax binder or not. Whatever you do, don't use completely blank sheets because you need some form of guide even if only ruled lines.

These designs need not be detailed. You do not, for example, have to print by hand every word of each line, but you do need to show how many lines will be used, the length of each line and the distance between lines. At this stage, you should know what you want to say, and knowing the space that is available will help you say it better. A very common fault is to try to get too much in, and this applies particularly to business cards. The essentials of a business card are the name, address and telephone number, and anything else is of secondary importance. A good jobbing printer, asked to design and print your business cards, will ensure that these important features are prominent. If you design your own, the temptation is to be too clever, to have an elaborate logo, to use several fonts and sizes, so that you end up with a messy piece of display with the essential information hidden among the eye-catching trivia.

No firm set of rules can make you an expert in this business, but a few rules can help to avoid some of the errors that leap out of the pages of magazines so often these days. One of the first rules is that anything that you want to appear in a magazine, or anywhere that will be read by anyone other than yourself, should be well printed. This might seem obvious, but you will see work that has been done on a dot-matrix printer in draft mode, which suggests either the use of a desktop publishing package that was not intended for a dot-matrix printer, or a user who did not realise that better print modes were available. Look at such a piece of work and compare it with the results that can be obtained from smoothed mode with Fleet Street Editor.

If there is one rule that might be considered more important than any other, it is that you should not try to put out any *major* piece of publishing single-handed. You might think that this defeats the aims of desktop publishing which for the first time allows a lot of printing to be under the control of one hand, but the fact remains that if you write your own text, do your own publishing and printing and check your own work, there will be problems. Working single-handed, you never see your own mistakes because you read what you think you want to see, not necessarily what appears in front of your eyes. The most ridiculous mistakes can pass you by because you happen to be concentrating on something else at the time, and this is particularly true if you are doing all your reading on screen. For anything of more than a few words (and even for a few, if their format is important), make a draft print and read it carefully, away from the computer.

The first thing to be critical about is spelling and typing. It's most unlikely that you don't know how to spell 'the' but this does not prevent your nimble fingers typing it as 'teh', and since your brain will reassure you that you can't go wrong with simple words like this, you never notice the mistake unless you read word by word through a printed sheet. Typing errors are a very potent source of mistakes like this, and if you do not use a word processor that incorporates a spelling checker for your text, then you should type slowly and check a lot. In any case, you cannot rely completely on spelling checkers, because, just to take one example, if you type 'that' instead of 'than', the spelling checker will not help you because either word is correctly spelled. This is just another example of an error which only reading will detect, and if someone other than you does the reading, the chance of detection is much greater. Not everyone can read critically, unfortunately, and some of the glaring mistakes that sometimes appear in advertising copy are a tribute to the ability of the brain to make sense of things that the eye ought to have rejected.

Bad spelling is unfortunately predominant in a lot of desktop publishing output. In an age when even some road signs appear with misspellings, this is probably inevitable, but dictionaries are not expensive, and you can still buy copies of *Fowler's Modern English Usage*, so what's the excuse? It's not trivial, because bad spelling in a publication suggests that it need not be taken too seriously, since the publisher did not bother to check it well. If you know that your spelling is shaky, then, oddly enough, it's more likely that you will make fewer mistakes, because you will check more thoroughly. It's those of us who think that our spelling is perfect who are more likely not to notice mistakes simply because we don't think we could have made any. As Mark Twain noted, it's not what you don't know that causes harm, it's what you know that ain't so.

Hand in hand with spelling goes grammar. At one time, English grammar, and particularly the topic of parsing and analysis, was taught in all secondary schools. We have now reached the stage at which teachers of foreign languages complain that they cannot teach German or French grammar to students who know nothing of English grammar, and, conversely, overseas students who learn English as a foreign language all too frequently know more of its grammar than native speakers. The point that seems to cause the most confusion is the apostrophe. This ought to be used to show missing letters, often the letter i. In the phrase 'it's clear', the apostrophe indicates that this is a shortening of 'it is clear', and in the phrase 'Harry's book' the apostrophe means that this is a shortened version of 'Harry, his book'. The main source of trouble is the use of the possessive forms of 'it', 'who', 'her', 'their', 'our', 'your'. These *never* use an apostrophe, so that the phrase 'It brings its own worries' is correct, whereas 'It brings it's own worries' is not. If you find yourself typing who's, her's, their's, our's or your's, then stop and think, because you are probably doing wrong.

The second most common grating grammatical mistake is to fail to realise that the word 'me' is the correct objective case of 'I' at all times. If you don't know what an objective case is, you are probably a victim of school-induced illiteracy and aged under 40. What I mean is the incorrect use of I and me. People who would never dream of saying 'It was given to I' will quite cheerfully say 'It was given to you and I', as if the use of 'you' exempted the 'I' from being in its correct form. This type of mistake sounds bad enough in speech, but looks even worse in print because we expect print to reflect a reasonable standard of English (and we are speaking of the standard that was not uncommon for a 12-year-old at one time). There are very few rules in the English language, so that it does not seem unreasonable that you should not break them in a printed work.

The third most common error has nothing to do with spelling or grammar, and is simply ignorance of what a word means. How many times, for example do you see 'less' used in place of 'fewer'. 'Less' applies to a bulk quantity, like less coal produced, less grain shipped. 'Fewer' applies to number, like fewer cars, fewer cases of 'flu. You never see 'fewer coal' but you do see 'less cars' for some extraordinary reason! Also in this class you find fashionable words that seem always to be incorrectly used. One of these is 'prevaricate' which means to tell lies, and is confused with 'procrastinate', which means to delay, to put something off until the next day. Confusions like this lose us the use of two words that caused no confusion before. If all this sounds too much like the rule of the schoolmaster of old, remember that it's our language, and when words lose meaning and become confused, then we lose the ability to communicate with them. Can anyone now use prevaricate or procrastinate in the hope that the meaning will be correctly understood? The confusion would never have arisen if it had not appeared in print, and it would never have appeared in print if standards of literacy had not dropped. If our language ceases to serve as a way of communicating precisely what we mean, then it becomes useless. Other nations take care of their languages and there are many compelling reasons for us to do the same, not least the reason that English is a language spoken by a very large number of people.

Spelling and grammar are topics that can be checked, either by yourself or, preferably, by someone else as well, and they are also items for which you have ample guidance in the form of dictionaries and books of style, like Fowler's masterpiece. The appearance of print is a very different matter. You can lay down rules for the way that print should be arranged, and find that you have to break half of the rules within a couple of lines. Rules and guidelines for printing are like rules and guidelines for art, they give you a start, but need to be abandoned if they conflict with what you think looks good. Just as we celebrate the greatness of artists who have abandoned rules to strike out in a direction of their own, we also celebrate the work of typographers who have known when to bend rules in favour of better appearance of text. You can study examples to your heart's content and learn from them, you can learn what rules there are, but the final result depends critically on your keen eye and good taste. These are qualities that you have to nurture and develop for yourself.

Having said all that, might we look at a few rules? Perhaps if we call then guidelines you will feel less inhibited by them. Whatever type of publication you embark upon, you will still have to follow roughly the same methods to obtain something that looks good and will be a pleasure to read. We can set out a set of guidelines for these methods so that you can avoid absurd blunders, and yet at the same time have considerable freedom to develop the work as you think fit. The all-important rule is to look critically at a draft print. Designing the layout of a page when you are looking at a distorted screen picture is asking too much of even an experienced typesetter and unless you are using a PC clone with a Hercules card that permits a screen display that is in true proportions you should not attempt to make a final judgement on the basis of the screen image. The Page preview facility of Fleet Street Editor is a good guide to the layout of the page, but you still need a draft copy for your final judgement.

The first decision that you will have taken on your printing is the page size. A lot of printed material uses the A4 size, which, being a metric size, does not conveniently fit into the printers' inch scales. Fleet Street Editor assumes a maximum page size of 8.5" wide by 10.5" deep, with minimum margins that provide for copy running to 8" × 10", and this will fit comfortably in an A4 page. Another common format is A5, which is an A4 sheet folded halfway along the longer dimension. Many newsletters are printed in A5 format so as to permit the use of A4 turned sideways and then folded. Whatever size you aim for, you need to remember how margins will be used. If you are working with a newsletter or any other material that extends to more than one page, your margins will have to allow for the space taken up when the sheets are bound together. A few word processors allow you to alternate the margin width for even-numbered and odd-numbered sheets, but you have to do this for yourself with Fleet Street Editor. The rule (don't break this one!) is that a sheet bearing an odd number appears to the right hand side of the binding when it is lying open, and will have a large margin on the left hand side. The even-numbered sheets will lie to the left, and have a large right hand margin. You might, of course, specify equal margins on each side, but this loses you a lot of text space, so that attention to your even and odd numbered pages will normally be needed.

Once the page size has been fixed, you can start thinking about page layout, designing each page on a squared or lined sheet. A few newsletters may require little in the way of such design, but the more time you spend away from the screen the better the results when you start work. In any case, if a newsletter is so straightforward that it needs no design, is it going to be a good read? Now that we have the technical ability to make even the most esoteric newsletter appear well laid out and printed, why should we assume that the subject matter is so gripping that the readers will put up with any old thing? The experience of computer user groups is that readers soon desert a poorly produced newsletter in favour of more professional work, and there is no reason why this experience should be unique. If your newsletter does not look good, someone else might do better.

The main item to decide about layout is whether you will go for one or more columns. My own feeling is that most newsletters on A5 paper should use only one column, because two-column work on paper this size looks too fussy. Even on A4, the use of two columns is not absolutely necessary unless the page consists of a lot of very short items. For a newsletter as distinct from a newspaper, the items will probably be longer, and you lose space by having two columns. Provided that the print is broken up here and there by an illustration, there need be no real objection to using a single column in A4. If your readers are predominantly elderly, there is a good case for aiming for the largest size that looks reasonable in the font you are using, so as to make for maximum legibility.

Your next decision is that of fonts. Avoid the use of too many fonts, because this is visually confusing. There is no good reason, in fact, for using more than one good font on a newsletter, particularly when you have the range that a font like New York offers. Too much variation in sizes and styles is almost as bad as too many fonts, and you should plan to have at most three sizes in most of your work. This might consist of 24 point for headlines, 18 point for sub-headings, and 12 or 10 point for the main text. Once again, remember that despite the name of your program, you are not trying to vie with ghosts of Fleet Street. Use bold for emphasis and italics for quotations by all means, but only a few words per page should need to be emphasised, and more than one paragraph in italic becomes tiring to read. Advertising work, of course, needs a greater visual impact. The problem with any advertising is that no-one reads it for pleasure, and everyone has become accustomed to the visual tricks in advertising material. The shorter the message, the more likely it will get across, but putting it into a large size or a fancy font does not guarantee that it will be noticed. Your eye has to be the judge here, and the selection of the larger fonts shown in Chapter 5 might give you some ideas.

Whatever you do, try to avoid making changes to fonts or sizes in the middle of any piece of text. This is very noticeable, and many readers interpret it as a change from one piece of text to another. This means that half of your readers will read down as far as the change, and the other half will start reading the page at the point of the change. You can use the change deliberately as a means of separating sections, but it is better to confine this to the first capital letter of each new section. You can, for example start each story with a capital letter in a larger size, possibly also of a different style or font, to act as a marker, so that a reader has no problem in identifying the correct start of each section. This is preferable to the common practice in typed newsletters of leaving a large gap between sections.

Large gaps brings us to white space, the appearance of blank paper. Too much white space is an abomination in any publication, and indicates that little or no thought as been put into the design. By contrast, overcrowded text is just as bad, and as much a deterrent to reading. You should think of white space as a splash of colour on your page, and try to balance it as well as possible. The worst offence is the fully justified line with two or three short words in it, and a large space between words. For this reason, it's often better to specify left justification only in your Page definition, and to put in full justification later with the Baselines menu. In this way, if you find that you have a line that looks bad with full justification, you can revert to left-justification. Some work might even look better with only left justification, using hyphens to split words so that the line lengths, though ragged, are reasonably similar.

You should not, however, be tempted to fill in white space with anything that comes to hand. If you have too much white space, that's a defect of planning, and you will not put it right by after-thoughts. If you have time, then get back to the drawing-board; if not, then get to work on the screen so as to make the page more acceptable. Perhaps some editing would help. For newsletter editors, editing only too often means cutting and correcting, but at times a longer headline can be a useful way of balancing up the appearance of a page. White space is more of a problem for a wide-page single column publication than for a multi-column one, because when you use more than one column you are less likely to have large gaps remaining. Don't, however, be tempted to put anything into the gutter between columns. A few desktop publishing users like to put lines down gutters, but this never looks good and can be very distracting to the eye.

Sometimes, it will be your sad duty to cut text. If you are running an 8-page newsletter, you can't let text spill on to a ninth page, and cutting is the only answer. Even careful planning can't avoid this at times, and you find that you have to pull back a line of two. Some reduction of white space may help, but you may still be left with the need to cut down text. This does not have to be the text that spills over, however. It may be that the article on pages 3 and 4 contained some repetitions that could be edited to a more concise form, and you can then shift text back until the whole newsletter is neatly filled. Making your newsletter of the same size each month (week, quarter, whatever) is an art-form in itself, and you should keep odd items of text around to fill in space if at any time you find that you are short of text. A gross excess will have to be dealt with by leaving an article over until the next issue, and small excesses can be dealt with by cutting text.

Other work

Because so much of desktop publishing is used for newsletters, it's easy to lose sight of the many other useful applications. Business uses are important applications of desktop publishing, and at the price levels we are considering, small businesses have a lot of uses for desktop publishing. A small business may not be able to afford elaborate layout for advertisements in newspapers, nor expensive glossy brochures. If, however, advertising can be presented as camera-ready copy to a 'free' newspaper, then the creation of the advertisement, which is normally the expensive part, has cost you nothing in cash (though it certainly costs in terms of time) and the hard-earned cash can go to ensuring maximum circulation for the advertising. The balance of time against money has to be remembered, but many small businesses have much more trouble with cash flow than with time allocation, and a few hundred pounds saved can be a considerable bonus, even if it is bought at the price of a Sunday evening spent at the keyboard.

Brochures are not so simple. Many advertising brochures are glossy and costly, but this does not ensure that they are widely read. It may be that a full technical specification of your product is needed for a few potential customers, or that you need more than one page to demonstrate why a customer should go for your services rather than those of someone else. Always ask yourself just how much the customer needs to read, and if it could not be put more succinctly. Leave the glossy pages to the large corporations and the suppliers whose mark-ups can pay for such things. Publish specifications by all means, perhaps quotations from satisfied customers, but always remember that most advertising material is unread, and what is read is often forgotten. One memorable phrase is worth many pages of bright but pointless photos or of descriptive but unread prose.

The ideal work for desktop publishing is the one-page advertising flyer. This is the challenge for you to put over what you can supply in a few words, and arranging these words in a limited space so that they make impact. If your message can be taken in at a glance, then it is much more likely to succeed than a mass of text whose message is concealed somewhere in the middle. Flyers can be disposed of much more cheaply than other forms of advertising, whether along with free circulation newspapers or handed out to shoppers, put through letterboxes or posted. If you can target upon your potential customers, then direct mailing can be very rewarding; if your users are likely to be anyone who sees the material, then hand-outs can bring in a significant amount of business.

You should, of course, design your own letterheads and business cards once you have the confidence to do so. If the creation of a logo is beyond you, remember that you can farm out such work, and you can specify that the result is to be delivered in the form of an ART file for Fleet Street Editor. More and more specialists are getting into the business of catering for the growing desktop publishing market with services such as video camera scanning and other conversions of material into files suitable for various desktop publishing packages. If you need to use a lot of material that is in the form of line drawings, you might consider the purchase of a low-cost scanner for yourself, but this is a step that needs a lot of consideration and which you would have to ensure was suitable. At the time of writing, the cost of a scanner, which converts a line drawing into a *large* disk file, was comparable with the cost of a good dot-matrix printer, and when you are working on a shoestring you can't contemplate such costs. If you have an intermittent need to scan line drawings, you might be able to hire a scanner. If, of course, the line drawings are simple you may be able to reproduce them on screen, using the line drawing tool. It is simpler, when you do this, to ignore the screen distortion, and make a copy as near to the scale of the original as possible; it helps if the size of the drawing can take up most of the screen area. You can then stretch the drawing in the vertical direction so as to make the printed copy of the correct scale. At the same time, you might want to reduce the overall dimensions, but always print a draft copy before proceeding any further. Most drawings made in this way will have to be adjusted with Magnify before they are finally ready to be saved as an ART file.

Final stages

The result of all your desktop publishing effort is one or more pages which form a master copy. By definition, users of desktop publishing on a shoestring do not print out with laser printers, even with the prices of some of these printers now promising to move below the £1000 mark soon, and you will need to give some thought as to how your efforts are to be communicated to the masses. However, one way to achieve a master copy of very high standard is to make use of bureau services which will supply your copy from a laser printer at about £1.50 per page. Some of these bureaux will even accept text sent along telephone lines. If you have difficulty in finding such a bureau your dealer may be able to help – or even provide the service – or you may get it done by one of the many instant print shops.

Some educational users have the easiest method available to them – the use of an overhead projector. You can buy blank transparencies for an overhead projector that can be printed on by a dot-matrix printer, and these blanks can be used in place of paper for a printout in smoothed mode. Placing each page in turn on the overhead projector then allows you to display the complete page to a class, and if the screen is large enough, class sizes of 20 to 60 can be catered for.

If you are working with this form of projection in mind, you have to avoid elaborate drawings or tiny fonts, because the result has to be readable on the screen from the remotest point in the class room or hall. This calls for considerable experience, because you have to know how large the space is and what size of screen will be in use. Always err on the side of clarity, because you will lose less by having to split your information into several pages than by having too much on one page. Remember also that you can work with overlays, printing supplementary material on another page which can be

Final Words **127**

placed over the first page to be viewed together.

For most users, however, the output will have to be on paper, and the intended number of copies may be from 5 to 500. A small readership can be coped with by using a photocopier. If you can get the use of a photocopier for about 1.5p per page, which is the going rate for a non-profit making copier, then small circulation numbers of newsletters can be reproduced in this way. Many church magazines are photocopied, using a machine that has been bought second-hand from an office supplier, and for which only the consumables like toner and belts have to be bought. If you had to use coin-slot copiers at 5p or more per copy, this would be suitable for very small numbers only, but at the lower rates, newsletter numbers can be as many as you can cope with copying. If, for example, you can use the photocopier at 1.5p per A4 page, and your newsletter is in A5 format, using four folded A4 pages, then the cost per newsletter is only 6p each, no matter how many or how few you duplicate.

Many users of desktop publishing will have access to an old ink duplicator such as the Gestetner or Roneo, using wax stencils. It is quite feasible to cut these wax stencils with a dot matrix printer (with the ribbon removed), and though the results are not always ideal, they are usually readable. The main snag is that wax stencil sheets, usually of the old foolscap size, do not always feed evenly through a printer, and are so far not available with perforated edges for tractor feed. This form of printing, however, permits very low-cost operation, because duplicating paper is very cheap, particularly when bought from a wholesaler such as Millway Stationery. If your main concern is getting out a newsletter to a large number of people at minimum cost, this is probably your best choice, but the quality of print is never likely to be first class.

The method that is needed for good quality reproduction, and which is essential for headed paper and business cards, is offset litho. The principle is a very old one, that ink made with an oil base will not adhere to water-wet surfaces. The name 'lithography' comes from the Greek word for a stone, because early lithography operated using a flat stone surface. If a mirror-image copy is made in ink on a stone, and the stone is then moistened, then when you run an inked roller over the stone the ink is deposited only on the parts which have already been coated in ink. A piece of paper laid on the stone can then be pressed down by another roller, and when the paper is stripped off it will retain a perfect impression of the master copy. This assumes, of course, that the stone is perfectly flat, and that the ink is free from lumps.

The use of stone has been consigned to the Stone Age, although stone lithography is still a medium for artists, and modern lithography is of the offset variety. This means simply that the text which is to be used as the master copy is not prepared on the material which is used for lithography. Modern small offset machines, such as the A.B. Dick, use either metal or plastic masters, and these are prepared from your pages of text using a form of photocopier. There are now some laser printers which can prepare such masters directly – remember that the printing on the masters must be a mirror-image of the original. Once a master is made, it can be used on a small lithographic rotary or flat-bed press at very low cost. The cost is so low that the method is used in educational work (sometimes, alas, to make unauthorised and therefore illegal copies from textbooks in contravention of copyright), and the cost of the masters is also low.

Offset litho can be viable for as few as 10 copies, and is economical for large numbers. It gives much clearer copies than the older type of ink duplicator and the master is much less fragile than a wax stencil, and has a longer working life. Whether this is applicable to your own uses depends on what is available. The educational user of desktop publishing will in all probability have access to offset litho equipment either in school, at a teachers' centre, or at a local technical college. The small-business user of desktop publishing can seek out a printer who will make litho copies of designs for headed paper, business cards, advertising literature and brochures. It is less likely, however, that the church or scout group will have access to this equipment, and the choice of duplicating methods is very much a matter of what can be obtained at lowest cost.

One of the least costly methods is also one of the least satisfactory and the most difficult to use for acceptable results. This is the spirit duplicator, for long the bane of school staffrooms. A good model of spirit duplicator, well maintained and fed with good quality masters can produce a small number of acceptable copies. This combination of circumstances is so rare, however, that most users associate spirit duplication with unreadable blue print on smudged paper. The problem is that the machine requires sympathetic handling, and since its use in schools is generally to produce material when there is only 5 minutes to spare, and with a master that has already been used to run off three batches in previous years, the poor results that are so familiar to use are hardly surprising.

For desktop publishing purposes, the dot-matrix printer can be used to prepare a spirit master directly. The glossy paper master is held against the copy paper (almost always blue, since this colour appears to give better reproduction) and the combination is fed into the printer. You need to experiment to some extent to find how best to make the copy. Some users remove the printer ribbon, but this usually allows the master paper to be perforated unless you can regulate the printer to reduce the impact of the needles. Your master copy should not use small fonts, because the process of duplication will exert a smoothing effect that will almost obliterate a small font. Even a typewritten master can appear far from sharp, and in some fonts, you might have to use 14 point to achieve really legible results. When your spirit master is ready, it can be used on the duplicator, but you can expect the print quality to be noticeably lower after about 30–50 copies, depending on the quality of the materials that you are using.

Final words

You should by now have a good working knowledge of Fleet Street Editor and how it can allow you to get into desktop publishing at rock-bottom prices. The most important feature of Fleet Street Editor from this point of view is that it is easy to use and about as foolproof as a piece of software can be. In many ways, it is even easier to use than most word processors, and yet it can yield copy, even using a 9-pin dot-matrix printer, that is clear enough for all but the most demanding applications.

Simplicity of use is important, because complicated packages seldom are used correctly or to anything but a fraction of their potential. The main attraction of Fleet Street Editor is that you can load it in and get working without needing to take a 30-minute revision course each time. When a desktop publishing package is easy to use, it gets used, and this is certainly something that can be said for Fleet Street Editor. The rest now is up to you. Spend as much time as you can looking at examples of well printed material, and think how you can apply the same principles to your own work. Together, you and Fleet Street Editor can considerably raise the reputation of low-cost desktop publishing.

Appendix A
Fleet Street Editor and Machines

The *Fleet Street Editor* program exists in versions for the BBC Micro, the Amstrad CPC 6128, and also for IBM PC and close compatibles. Of these, the IBM version offers fewest restrictions of memory, though the version of the Amstrad CPC 6128 is very similar. Other versions are differently named, so that the version of Fleet Street Editor for the Amstrad PCW 8256 and PCW 8512 is called *Editor Plus*, and the considerably enhanced version for the Atari ST is called *Fleet Street publisher*. The following table (reproduced courtesy of Mirrorsoft Ltd) summarises the differences among the versions.

Appendix A

FACILITY	VERSION	FLEET STREET EDITOR BBC	FLEET STREET EDITOR CPC	FLEET STREET EDITOR IBM	EDITOR PLUS PCW	PUBLISHER 1 ATARI ST
Text Handling						
WYSIWYG		√	√	√	√	√
Text processing		√	√	√	√	√
Bulk text entry			√		√	√
ASCII file acceptance		√	√	√	√	√
Wordwrap		√	√	√	√	√
Justification		√	√	√	√	√
Hyphenation						√
Kerning						√
Variable leading			√	√	√	√
Widows and orphans						√
Search and replace						√
Tabulation & Indentation						√
Multiple fonts		√	√	√	√	√
Multiple point sizes & styles			√	√	√	√
International character sets		√		√	√	√
Editable fonts		√			√	√
Accepts laser fonts				√		√
Inverse type		√	√	√	√	√
Grey scale						√
Picturewrap		√	√	√	√	
Graphics Handling						
Graphics library supplied		√	√	√	√	√
Boxes & Rules available		√	√	√	√	√
Advanced graphic tools		√	√		√	√
Accepts scanned images				√		√
Accepts graphics from other packages		√	√	√	√	√
Page Make-up Handling						
Full page composition			√	√	√	√
Automatic page numbering					√	
Text editing in page make-up			√	√	√	√
Graphics handling in page make-up			√	√	√	√
Picture sizing/cropping in page make-up				√	√	√
Picture blocks			√	√	√	√
Linked blocks to same page			√	√	√	√
Linked blocks to nominated page					√	
Snap to guides					√	√
Left and right hand page orientation					√	√
Multiple page sizes				√	√	√
Variable margins				√	√	√
Bastard columns				√	√	√
Editable page dummies				√	√	√
Style sheets						√
Output						
Dot matrix drivers		√	√	√	√	√
Laser printer drivers				√		√
Postscript drivers				√		√
Other typesetter drivers						√
System Requirements						
Minimum memory		32K	128K	512K	256K	520
Minimum drive configuration		1 Floppy	1 Floppy	2 Floppy	1 Floppy	1 Floppy
		£39.95/ £44.95	£39.95	£183.99 (version 3)	£49.95	£125.00

Appendix B
Some Useful Addresses

Mirrorsoft Ltd,
Headway House,
66/73 Shoe Lane,
London EC4P 4AB.
Tel: (01) 377 4645

Fleet Street Editor
(Fleet Street Editor for PC and PCW is available in all Dixons Business Centres and the Tandy Business Points.)

The Electric Studio Products Ltd,
Unit 8, The Cam Centre,
Wilbury Way,
Hitchin,
Herts. SG4 0TW.
Tel: (0462) 420222

Light pen and other graphics devices including video camera.

Millway Stationery,
Chapel Hill,
Stansted,
Essex CM24 8AP.
Tel: (0279) 812009

Stationery for reprographics

PW Computer Supplies,
Dawlish Drive,
Pinner,
Middlesex HA5 5LN.
Tel: (01) 868 9548
     (01) 866 2258

Printers, ribbons, paper, software, accessories.

PDSig,
1500a Greenford Road,
Greenford,
Middlesex UB6 0HP.
Tel: (01) 864 2611

Software interest group for PC supplies low-cost software like PC-ART, Finger Paint etc.

Wordstream Ltd,
Wordstream House,
St Aldhelms Road,
Poole BH13 6BS
Tel: (0202) 752155
Fax: (0202) 752216

Tandy UK Ltd,
Tandy Centre,
Leamore Lane,
Bloxwich,
Walsall WS2 7PS

Laser bureau services.
(Can accept text by way of Mirror communications program and a suitable modem.)

Appendix C
Laser Printers and Page-description Languages

A laser printer is a development of the familiar electrostatic photocopier of the Xerox (TM) variety. In an electrostatic copier, the original paper is pressed against a material which is electrically an insulator until it is struck by light. This material is electrically charged, making it able to attract small particles, and then the master copy is illuminated. This makes the material conduct where the light has reached it, so that the electric charge leaks away except in the dark areas, which will be the inked areas of the original. A dry powder ink (toner) will now stick to these ares when blown over the plate, and this pattern of dry ink can be transferred to a clean sheet of paper. Finally, the paper with its dry ink is passed under a heater which melts the powdered ink into the paper, leaving a permanent copy.

In a laser printer, the removal of the electric charge from an insulating plate is carried out by a laser beam, and this laser beam is under the control of a separate computer which is built-into the printer. Unlike ordinary computer printers, the laser printer deals not with characters, or lines, but pages. The principle is that the appearance of each dot on a complete sheet is held in the memory of the printer, and the printing is therefore very fast, about 8 seconds for a complete A4 page. This implies that a laser printer needs a large memory, because the definition can be very good, of the order of 300 dots per inch. For a piece of paper measuring 8" × 10", this implies that the memory must hold information on the state of 7,200,000 dots. Since the memory must also hold the state of the page in ordinary form (as a set of ASCII or other codes), this means that a lot of memory is needed. The minimum memory for a laser printer is 512K, and many offer 1Mbyte or more.

Laser printers can be divided into two types, those which offer page description languages and those which do not. The simpler and cheaper laser printers are in use rather similar to dot-matrix printers, and can produce results that do not look all that much better if you drive them from a page in draft mode. If your laser printer could cope only with printing a dot on paper for each dot on the screen, then the results would be very poor indeed, and the purpose of the laser support fonts is to be able to send a much finer pattern of dots to the printer than you can from the ordinary fonts. Incorrect font use explains why so much work from laser printers looks little better than from dot-matrix printers, and some looks even worse. Many laser printers can be set to emulate the print of popular daisywheel or dot-matrix printers (like the Diablo 630 and the Epson FX), and some offer their own fonts, either built-in or in the form of plug-in cartridges. Fleet Street Editor V.3.0 incorporates many more facilities for controlling laser printers.

The most expensive laser printers offer a page description language which on most examples is a programming language called PostScript. The use of PostScript means that the actions of the printer can be controlled by commands that are sent along with text, and these printers offer the highest quality of print that is obtainable using desktop publishing. To use them to advantage, however, you need to know the PostScript language, which is not quite so simple as a computer programming language like BASIC, and for this reason, together with the price of such machines, makes printers of this type the choice of the professional typesetter who will set master copies for you from your original disk files.

Even the quality of a laser printer is regarded by many as insufficient for the reproduction of photographs. This is mainly because of the absence of half-tones on most laser printers, but their use is also criticised on the grounds that only 300 dots per inch is too small for good reproduction of an image. A lot depends on what you expect to achieve. A TV picture, for example, uses a set of 600 lines no matter what size of screen is used, and for colour pictures will give a resolution of only 300 lines (because the contents of pairs of lines are averaged). A resolution of 300 lines on 24" of screen is equivalent to 12.5 dots per inch, which makes the 300 dots per inch of the laser printer look like a very high definition indeed.

Index

10/12 point Times, 27
24-pin printer, 2
90 degree turns, 70

ABODES.MAC, 67
Adana hand-press, 1
add-on cards, 10
additional font disks, 19
addresses, 132
adjust baselines, 33
advertising, 125
advertising flyers, 109
alterations, 31
analysis, 120
APLASER.FNT, 115
apostrophe, 120
Apple Macintosh, 64, 97
.ART file, 64
Art menu, 71
art outline box, 65
artwork, 64
ASCII code, 37
AUTOEXEC.BAT file, 11
automatic hyphenation, 35

Baselines menu, 32
bastard columns, 52
black pencil, 90
bold type, 4, 18
Bombay font, 92
box drawing, 51
brochures, 125
bubble, 101
built-in fonts, printer, 2
business card, 104, 125
business uses, 124
butler example, 65

CAD programs, 113
Cairo font, 19, 44
Calgary font, 109
camera-ready copy, 3, 7, 125
Center, baselines, 32
centring line, 32
change leading option, 34
changing fonts, 123
Clipboard, 39
clubs, 117

colour, 10
colour monitors, 11
columns, 25, 122
columns by spacing, 59
COLUMNS-3.MAC, 75
computer image, 97
Copy, 40
Courier font, 17, 57
creating batch file, 16
cross-wires pointer, 51
cursor, 23
cursor and font, 45
cursor shift, columns, 47
Cut, 40
cutting text, 124

damaged letters, repair, 104
decorated letters, 102
Decorative fonts, 110
Define Page, 25
definition box, 66, 74
deleting graphics text, 86
dimension checking, 108
disk capacity, 13
DISPLAYS.MAC, 75
distortion, resizing, 68
distortions of letters, 84
distribution disks, 11
doctoring images, 90
document design, 118
dot-matrix printer, 2
draft print, 30
dragging, 23
duplicate image, 67

editing art images, 95
editing graphics text, 86
Editor Plus, 2
Electric Studio Products, 98
electrostatic copier, 134
embedded codes, 45
emphasis, 123
equipment, 1
erase along line, 91
eraser, 90
erasing square, 70
Executive fonts, 109
extending baseline, 49

Index **137**

extracting artwork, 65

F program, 37
F-key use, 8
Fleet Street Editor, 8
flip commands, 69
flyer, 125
font, 1, 5, 123
FONTMOVE, 19
Fonts disk, 14, 16
fonts on hard disk, 22
fonts, variety, 17
footer, 41
French manuscript, 102
FRENCH.MAC, 102
FSE directory, 11
full justification, 26
    columns, 48
fully justified text, 3

Gem, 9
getting started, 23
gothic letters, 44
grammar, 120
graphics cards, IBM, 10
graphics text, 57, 81
graphics text editing, 86
grey letters, 28
grid, 108
    pattern, 71
guidelines, 121
gutter, 26
    size, 47

half-click, 9
hand pointer, 66
hand-press, 1
handles, 32, 46, 68
handwriting simulation, 92
hard-disk installation, 11
headed paper, 108
header, 41
headline for columns, 48
Heidelberg font, 111
Hercules card, 23
HPLASER.FNT, 115
hyphenation, 35

ignorance of words, 121
image position, 71
image sizes, 67
images and messages, 99
imported text, 36
indenting, 33
indicator bar, 23
individual letters, 88
ink duplicator, 1, 127
inserting box, 56
installation, 10
inversion, 83
inverted image, 72
italic style, 18

Jump to Page option, 38

justification, 33

kerning, 117
keys, cursor movement, 23

laser fonts, 115
laser printer, 2, 7, 134
laser printer bureau, 126
layout plan, 55
layout, page, 122
leading, 27
left justification, 26
letterhead, 43, 125
light-bulb image, 96
light-pen, 98
line thickness choice, 50
line tool, 50
literacy, 121
lithography, 127
LocoScript, 118
logo, 104

.MAC extension, 30
.MAC files, 64
Magnify command, 93
manual, Fleet Street Editor, 8
margin change, 44
marginal notes, 60
margins, 26
marking text block, 32
measurement of type size, 18
memory, laser printer, 134
merging images, 74, 95
message in bubble, 101
mirror images, 70
monochrome display, 11
mouse, 8
    button, 9
    cursor, 28
    dragging, 9, 65
    pointer, 23
    writing, 92
MOUSE.COM, 12
mouse/keys choice, 25
Move in Steps, 71, 108
multiple columns, 46

NEW file name, 31
new Fonts disk, 19
New York font, 18, 28
numbers, page, 122

objective case, 120
offset litho, 127
overflow, 39
overhead projector, 126

page boundaries, graphics text, 81
page description language, 135
page preview, 29
page size, 122
page to page movement, 71
parsing, 120
Paste, 40

138 Index

PC-compatible, 2
PCW machines, 2
pencil action, 90
penguins, 70
photocopier, 127
photographic negative, 72
photographs, 135
PictureWrap, 77, 112
pixels, 95
planning, 24
point size, 18
pointless image, 85
possessive forms, 120
PostScript, 135
POSTSCRIPT Times font, 18
pound sign, 39
PPC 640, 10
print page, 29
print to disk file, 42
PRINT.DEF file, 14
printer ribbon prices, 2
PRINTER.EXE, 14
proportional spacing, 5
.PUB file, 24

Quadrille paper, 118
Quebec font, 109

Realign text, 36
reflection in water, 85
resize image, 68
retouching, 69
right justification, 26, 43
right-hand margin, 3
RPED editor, 13
ruler lines, 67
ruler scales, 46

sans serif, 6
saving file, 30
saving text, 61
scaling image, 67
scanner, 125
screen displays, 112
screen distortion, 23
selecting faces, 29
separating merged images, 75
serif, 6
set-up instructions, 10
shadow text, 88
shaped columns, 56
shifting baselines, 53
short lines, 35
side tools, 50
single sheet printing, 29
single-handed work, 119
single-page work, 39
size, horizontal, 105

size/style combinations, 28
smoothed print mode, 30
SNAP2ART, 113
SNAPSHOT, 113
software, 7
solid black, 84
space for artwork, 112
spaces, mixed fonts, 45
spacing, 33
spacing graphics letters, 82
spelling check, 37
spelling checkers, 119
spirit duplicator, 128
squared paper, 118
start-up disk, 16
stencilled lettering, 103
stepped image, 104
store, layout, 34
style, 6, 118
styles, 18
system disk files, 14

tabulation, 57
tabulation key, 57
text block change, 31
text cursor, 28
Text justify, 26
text/graphics merge, 77
Times font, 115
tracking, 117
two-column work, 46
.TXT extension, 31, 37
type size, 18
typing errors, 119
typing page, 28
typing speed, 29

underlining, 4, 50
uniform spacing, 5
US names, fonts, 19

variety of fonts, 17
versions, Fleet Street Editor, 130
video camera, 99

Western Digital disk, 11
white pencil, 90
white space, 123
widows, 117
word processing, 3
words and images, 76
WordStar, 4
wrapping by spacing, 81

Xerox, 134

zeroing baseline, 52